THE
SILENT
CURSE
II

TSC II:
STILL CURSING,
SIGNED KARMA

Authored by

ASHLEIGH S.
WILKERSON

Dedicated to my gorgeous Grandma "Grandmawww" Pauline McFall and my amazing cousins Tyajah A. Anderson, Latrice Jackson, & Kimberly Evans

TABLE OF CONTENTS

ACKNOWLEDGEMENT

I'd first like to acknowledge GOD... Thank you for blessing every word, for your continuous guidance, and for all your love.

Everything will **always** be because of you.

And to **EVERYONE** that read **The Silent Curse,** or who have shared words of encouragement, supported in any way, shape, or form... From the bottom of my heart <u>I Thank You</u>.

PRELUDE

The doorbell rings and Mariah walks over in her red fleece pajama set and fuzzy black slippers. Her hair is in a high bun minus the curls that slid out from the back, her blanket is wrapped around her shoulders, and she still hasn't put her glasses on yet. They don't help much, so she hardly ever wears them anyway. The kitchen smells like coffee, and the biscuits she forgot she was cooking. She was multitasking a bit, cleaning the bathroom, the living room, and the den when she noticed a story in the newspaper. She crouched down by the tub and began reading. She was easily sidetracked. Even though, this visit came as no surprise –once she was in her busy body mood there was really no sitting still. She starts to scurry feeling as if the house is a mess. A mess in her case means her jacket is on the sofa, and a magazine is out of place on her rack or a pen is on her desk instead of in the holder next to her calculator. She's so particular, everything is a bother especially when she's pressed for time.

Oh, yes... Today, April 12th, 2015, she's scheduled for part two of her documentary at 12:12 p.m. with award winning Journalist – Justyce McCall. Part one left everyone speechless. She gave so much without giving anything at all. The audience was hanging onto her every word and in disbelief that she could have experienced such traumatizing events. Justyce wasn't a slouch himself. His expressions never wavered. Most agree that his body was relaxed the entire time. No sign of any opinion. He was a pro and anyone that had the opportunity to view the special in its entirety could attest. The public has since been begging for more information about Mariah Shante Beauvoir. Every news company in the south wants a piece of what Justyce accomplished. Their discussion flowed so well and almost without any effort from either party. She wanted to speak, and he wanted to listen. Movie critics even ranted about Justyce's etiquette, they were eager to know how exactly he convinced Mariah to give up such vivid details. Some even mentioned possible deals if only Justyce would share his magic or at least give a second dose that was just as good or better. Humbly, Justyce stated during a radio interview with 98.2 KYSS FM just two weeks after the original airing that "the secret to an amazing interview is all about defining and building a personal connection."

Mariah enjoyed the documentary and working with Justyce McCall so much that she made it clear that she wants to continue with no one else except for him. She told fans and spectators that more important than delivering her story, is the person it's delivered through. Rumor has it she personally thinks Justyce is hot but he is kind of too young for her. It's never been confirmed but a source said they saw them share a little more than dinner. Her signature meal is penne and vodka, and that's exactly what they had that evening. What a coincidence right? She called it a thank you, and a celebration meeting. She was furious when asked about it. She swore up and down that it was some sort of conspiracy against her out of hatred for the way in which she turned her life around. She started to say some pretty hateful things about the blogger that leaked the details and that's when she reiterated the fact that she will speak with no one else except for Justyce. She said the young intern at the time that created the fictional gossip was incompetent and shouldn't have said anything without legit facts. It was rather strange, like most people would say it's a lie, it's a fabricated story, so why did she get her panties in such a bunch over something she swore had no way of being true? The doorbell rings three more times all in a row. She's walked toward and away from it about nine times now in between spotting a new chore. Unfortunately, she couldn't save the biscuits. She took them out, and let them sit on the counter, but they were much tanner than usual. A hard pounding knock, one final ring, and a soft yet aggravated voice yells out hello. As Mariah finally opens the newly fixed door she's greeted with a surprise.

"Good morning, can I help you?" asked Mariah. Before her is a young woman approximately in her mid to late twenties. She's average height with dark brown almost black hair, brown eyes and milk chocolate skin. She has on a long beige trench coat, denim jeans, beige knee-high boots, a matching sweater, and a clipboard with the initials R.T. on the back. She seems welcoming, yet her face says she can turn things upside down with the snap of a finger. "Hello I hope I'm not disturbing you," said The Woman. "My name is Rebecca Townsend. Justyce McCall is my partner. He's been out for a few days however my supervisor asked that I come in his place. I'm looking for A... Mariah S. Beauvoir."

"Hello there, I know who you are dear." said Mariah. "I recognize you from the office. I've stopped in a few times for follow up discussions. I'm sure you realize you've found me. Not to be rude, but isn't it part of your job to become familiar with your subjects especially if they've been in your company before? How is it that I instantly remembered you but you didn't recognize me? How long have you worked in the field? Are you college educated? I imagine you're not as old as you appear. Don't mind me, I'm just not one for sudden change you know. The information I've shared with Justyce holds dear to my heart. Why didn't they notify me of this last-minute change? It's a lovely gesture of you all but shouldn't I have been asked first? I thought I made myself clear... he's the only one I want to discuss anything with. Have you viewed the first video? Have you ever created a documentary of your own? I'm sure you're at least aware of the praise it received, I'd like to continue on that same path. Do you have any work that I could take a look at? How about a resume? Come on you have to give me something! How do I even know you're qualified for this type of story? Sorry, that probably came out totally wrong. I'm just being cautious and covering myself. Not to be disrespectful but I don't know if you will have my best interest at heart so it's all out of safety. There is no malicious intent, but I have a lot riding on the strength of this second interview. Producers and executives from multiple companies have already told me should this go over well and do greater numbers than the last, I just might be looking at my own television series. Can you get a load of that? Thanks to my actual life and the genius we call Justyce I've been able to appeal to those around my parents age and even mine, but it's you guys I'm really aiming for. This day and age it's the youth that has the greatest impact especially since all the technological advances you know stuff like that darn social media. I'm not really one for it. I know you're probably saying I sound older than I look. I had to be, I had to grow up much faster than most. My spirit has the ways of a woman in her 70's though. I still prefer to write everything out, do long division, and hold hour length phone conversations. Thank God for a great publicist and nieces that understand media outlets huh girl? Sorry for the tangent we could talk about this all day if you let me. Bottom line, I just want to make sure that this section is even more thought out than the first. You know I want to progress that's all. I mean do you see the upgrade in the house? Well you didn't get the chance to see before but look at this kitchen. You wouldn't think it were the same one from back in 1990 when my sisters and I stood by my mother watching her prepare meals. It's become my favorite space. I sit here at this small table and write for hours. I talk to the twins on three way almost every other day right here with my feet propped up. I'm not much of a cook. It's not that I can't, but it never appealed to me. Not personally, always just like to watch. But when I have guest I'll throw down and whip up something you thought would be on the cooking channel. That's all thanks to to the fame I've gained. It's given me visitors, and a reason to chef it up once in a while. Our hard work basically allowed me to step things up a lot in all aspects of life. You see the understanding he and I have? He knows how to give me what I want. He's earned my gratitude. So, if you can guarantee the same level of respect well then, I guess I might be in," said Mariah.

"It sounds like I have some big shoes to fill. Boy did he wow you. But no really, I'm honored to know that one of our own has pleased you in such a way. This means all of our extra hours of training and courses are definitely being implemented. However, I'm actually older than Justyce. Not by much, but I can call myself his elder. I guess my crazy schedule is adding to the bags under my eyes that you can't stop staring at. I'm sure that's what you're referring to in regards to my age right? Anyway, McCall and I studied together for quite some time. So, to answer your question, I am college educated. But my intelligence isn't limited just to my schooling. I've learned through my educators as well as different companies and hand on experiences before deciding to work for XYZ-8 News. I chose them. They were just one of twelve different offers I had at the time.

They stood out because of the way they reward their employees for their hard work. It's owned by a married couple. They work well together. They're very organized and I like that. I landed the position first, took over in our department and needed someone to fill my old role. I called on Justyce and he was more than willing to join the team. He's a wonderful Journalist. He keeps to himself, does each assigned task diligently, and never complains. He is normally my go-to person for everything. If there's a juicy story I know I can count on him to solve the mystery and bring the vision to life. He's an awesome story teller which is why he excels so well in the Features department. He's not a fan of video but as we both know it's becoming another niche of his. See, I do pay attention to detail. Since we began working together, he's only requested one day off until this morning. He left a message with the receptionist saying he has the flu and needs time to get to the Doctor. So here I am. And to answer your question, yes, I'm very much aware of the reviews for part one. I actually approved everything before the public had the opportunity to watch and or read. So, before you continue on fan girl, I do believe I helped a bit as well," said Rebecca.

"Well excuse the heck out of me Boss. I guess it'll have to be alright then now won't it? My days are hectic so there's no need to put off any more time. First impression I'll tell you I was about to slam the door right back in your face. But you didn't back down when I grilled you about your work experience. You shut me up real smooth if I do say so. You should feel great. I'm astonished, I wouldn't think you were running things. You know how some people just have that look? You don't have that. I feel like with time you'd soften up. That's a compliment too, there's nothing wrong with having a heart and being able to sympathize with others. I'm a bit like that myself. I'm a real personal kind of person. I also didn't know a woman co-owns the station. Now that is impressive. Again, my need to badger you is only for both of our well-being. I like to know who I'm getting involved with and letting into my privacy especially these days you know? I grew up in the 80's and the 90's so it's a whole different Raleigh let alone world out there today with all this computer stuff so you can't be so careful. I see some of these devices and it's absolutely terrifying how there's no hiding and just about everything can be tracked.

Don't give me that look either. I know I should be well adjusted right I'm not that old it's only 2015 which means if you're good with at least basic math then you guessed it darling I'm only 35. But we all have preferences, right? Maybe being out of touch with the outside for a bit stripped me of the learning others did when it came to the advances today. Or maybe not. I think either way I wouldn't be so interested in my telephone talking at me and answering my calls. I liked the beeper a lot. Anyway, if you look to the far end of my kitchen counter, you can see my vanilla candles and my PST board. It stands for positive self-talk. I visit it more often than one would think. Why? Well because how can I talk to others happily in an upbeat manner without speaking to myself in the same way. It's all about energy and finding balance. There's a connection through it and I want every energy that connects with mine to be positive. That's what I'm working on the most, understanding and weeding out gloomy energy. I bet you're wondering if I learned that from my therapist. I sure did. It's almost mind boggling the negative connotation that seeking an outside source of help has developed. Lots of individuals assume therapist means crazy and therapy is conditioning to keep you in a joyless state of mind. I say that's nothing but pure ignorance. I believe if you're walking around today without a counselor or some form of support especially trying to deal with the ways of this universe, you're the crazy one. Even the most respected individuals from all walks of life need a listening ear from time to time. It's easy to hear what you want, but how do you react when you hear what you need? When it's unbiased? When it's straight to the point? When the person really just cares about the issue and solely the issue? You'll be surprised a lot of people won't like that. So, with that being said let's have a little session of our own. Tell me a little about yourself. Where are you from? How about your folks, and how did you get your foot in the door to journalism," asked Mariah?

"Well it almost feels like I'm the one being interviewed. First, I'm never offended… Most people never know much about the significance of my role. I keep my title under wraps. Only feel the need to throw my weight around when I'm undermined. It's a competitive field. There isn't much room for ill feelings or anything of the sort. For the most part I take everything with a grain of salt. Genuine connections are rare to find. You are correct, energy can be very contagious. But I'm not here for us to spend weekends together shopping or playing tennis. I don't plan to get away or dish out my dirty laundry. I have few friends but I'm in no way looking to fill any extra positions. I'm really here to finish what you started. I think your age is what strikes me the most. To the average individual you're still incredibly young. For some reason you don't feel that way. I've heard you say on more than one occasion that you feel spiritually you've been here before or much older. That's different, most people want to be and feel young and keep up with the times. Most people have cell-phones and laptops. It seems like your only interest in things like technology or the advancement of social media and or blogs is for the increase of exposure for your documentary. And more about me…I'm just a few blocks away from you over on Brace Avenue. But I'm an army brat. My parents met while in the service. I was born in Korea and raised in North Carolina," replied Rebecca.

"Well that's splendid, just the attitude you'll need covering a tale such as mine. I'm sincere, but I won't sugar coat if you know what I mean. I've replayed every word in my head. Every word I'll share with you shall be memorized so if you choose to quote me, please be on point. I'm not sure if Justyce explained my way of doing things, but I take no mess and hate nothing more than my words being misconstrued. I'm no music video, please don't chop or screw with my content. One lie, one error, and your credibility is over and done with. You say you're his boss, so I expect his work times ten. Hand me your coat I can put it away for you if you'd like. Seems like your parents have something special if they're still together today. I reckon it was pretty fun traveling from place to place. You have a husband of your own, what about children," asked Mariah?

"Well, someone in your stance that seems to have such a love hate relationship with the media should also know a little more about the outlets before agreeing to such conferences. I'll have no problem with my quotes. But you should know the more you give, the more I can give back. My content will be nothing short of superb either way, but the way you are portrayed is solely based on you. My biggest job is to highlight your character That's something that I can't give nor take away from you. I'm not sure what sort of agreement you and Justyce had prior to today but I treat my career as most people treat their children. We're focused on you today, remember this is your voice not mine. My parents are like every other married couple. They're still together, but every day they are faced with a new lesson. I've asked them about traveling and how they made things work and they've both said in different ways that their marriage and bond worked because they both wanted it to. They said they never gave up and every day they both fall in love with the same person almost three decades ago. The outside changed with time but never the inside and they've always kept that in mind. I on the other hand am a single woman. I'm also childless. But I would like both one day," said Rebecca.

"Becky, are you creating a false theory about my prior interview experience? Is that sass I sense? Are you belittling me? You do know that's how rumors get the swirling especially amongst you reporters and news people. Have you heard that I hate rumors? Say exactly what you mean. See how simple I was able to bark at you? Don't go being a female dog. Besides Girl Justyce is just an acquaintance and its strictly business. We've officially worked together that's all. I took a big chance on him. I helped bring out the spark in him and look at where he is now. It's strictly platonic darling. You do realize there is a such thing like as in a man and woman working together without having to have any form of a physical encounter? I hope so otherwise I'd hate to ask how you get your promotions. Not that I'm in any position to judge or anything. And your parents give me hope. That is so deep I almost wanted to snap for them. You still haven't given me your coat yet. There's no need to hold it you can get comfortable. Ignore the lies, I don't bite all the time. It's okay to have a seat. My daddy always said sit down you'll make the house poor. Eh he also said he'd dance at my wedding.

Haven't had one of those yet though. I doubt he'd make it anyway." said Mariah.

"It's Rebecca Townsend…and no sass, all class. And I've moved up within my organizations just as you have. So, you take that as you choose to. In regards to my parents, thank you for the compliment I'll be sure to let them know the next time my mother calls me. I'll hold my coat here. You're still in your prime. Dreams come true. I'm sure your dad would do his best to make it there for your big day." said Rebecca. "Touché. Oh yeah, this will be fun. Please make yourself at home. I'll even let you have my favorite chair. You should feel special, I never allow anyone to sit in it. It used to be my father's. That was his rule, we were never allowed to sit in his chair. Well actually that wasn't quite the rule. Melody and Melissa could sit wherever they chose to. I wasn't allowed to sit in it. Do you like coffee? I just put some on. I made a treat too but from the strong scent rushing in I probably didn't cook them so well. Ok wait a second. I want you to be totally honest so I will too. I know for a fact that I didn't cook them well. But I've always liked my food well done anyway. What about you? My fiancé used to take care of all our meals. See I was close to taking that long walk down the aisle. It's not my favorite topic. It was really short lived. Now, I eat a lot of salads, and easy things to make. I'm always on the go anyway so there isn't much time," said Mariah.

"I'm okay, thanks for asking. I'm sorry about your fiancé. I actually heard about the news not too long ago. He was so young, and so talented. I wasn't planning on mentioning him unless you did first. But I did think about him when you said your father wouldn't be at your wedding. I know sometimes when things happen suddenly and so recently it can be frustrating to keep having to explain. Believe it or not we spoke once. He got one of our other clients off a few years back. His name was T.K. Wilson. He is a former basketball player for the Detroit Jets. He actually handled your case right and got you a pretty good deal? How long were you all together?" asked Rebecca.

"It felt like an eternity. You know he saved my life. We had so many plans and dreams we wanted to accomplish together. He was the only man I ever really trusted. And I meant that my father probably wouldn't be there regardless. Let's not harp on him right now. I'm sure you have more than enough questions related to him. Was your client guilty?" asked Mariah.

"That's very hard to take in. It must be difficult to manage at times. I don't mean to pry but on News 120 a show that airs in the evening, they said he died of a stroke and was immediately cremated. He seemed healthy. Was there such history in his family? And of course, being that you were engaged to a lawyer you're well aware of confidentiality and conflict of interest I'm sure," said Rebecca?

"No history at all…Dr. Pressleigh said it's rare but very possible. He could have been under stress during that time, or just anything you know freak accidents happen. Some things are just out of our control. And yes, aside from his parents and few cousins he didn't have very much family. His parents thought cremation would be best. And yes, I'm aware of the golden rule, but it was worth a shot. I'll take my guess and say he was as guilty as me huh," said Mariah.

"That's very true. Speaking of control, you've felt this way on more than one occasion. Isn't that right? In part one with Justyce, you kept mentioning a curse that you finally understood. You said you beat the curse, like some sort of game. Could you further explain? Also, you're right it was worth the shot but the rules are the rules. So please let's just keep our actual objective in mind and continue on with things. I will never ask you to compromise your integrity, so please don't ask me either," said Rebecca.

"Alright, since you put it that way, no problem. It's no secret that my mother hurt my Dad by having an affair with someone else. The timeline created doubts not only in my father's mind, but everyone's mind as well. The big question was if I were his or someone else's. So my father mended his ego and heart by resenting me. He became a coward, and my mother became a monster. Two people I thought I once knew, yet hadn't the slightest clue what either were capable of doing. To add a spin on things, my father was no saint himself... he also had an affair for twenty years. So, let me break it down for you, my mother hid a one-time affair for two decades, while my sly like Father deceived by her lustful encounter with another man lived two separate lives just mixing and mingling with this one and that for just as long. Yes, child I'm saying they are one in the same. My mother still swears until this day that she didn't do half of the things I discovered. She says someone framed her. Can you believe that? I feel so bad for her lack of self-esteem, I don't even bother to argue with her anymore. We rarely talk because I can't even stomach her excuses any longer. If she's not using my sisters and I as her reason for watching me get verbally abused by my father, she's looking for a way to make her scandal acceptable. She uses the time she spent locked away as guilt. But again, we all make choices. It was her fault the way in which she was placed in that predicament to begin with. Oh gosh I feel it coming on again. Sorry I'm getting off topic any who, that's the **first** part of the curse. I realize that **people aren't always who they say they are nor who we need them to be**. The **second** part is through all of that chaos, I somehow **fell madly in love with myself inside out**. This is the first time I'm really saying it out loud. I love myself, I love me. I'm seriously in love with all that I'm made up to be.

I don't think either of my parents understand what exactly that means. I don't think they ever truly loved each other. I don't think it was ever possible because they didn't love themselves first. I was never taught self-love. They weren't either, and I know it created doubt and caused them to hurt one another. Honestly, I don't think they were ever meant to even be together. Cross paths, maybe even spend a little time, but not a lifetime, not all of what occurred. So many people were hurt behind their actions. People lost their lives, went to prison, hell it's all why we're here together right now. I think had they caught on sooner that it's okay to love from a distance, a lot of time and energy would have been saved. Comfort and lack of self-esteem will have you stuck. I remember during one of their many altercations my mama was crying in the bathroom with the door barely cracked. She and daddy had argued a minute before and he stormed out after calling her a bunch of names.

During this particular time, he was asking about me again. When wasn't he? He said he started noticing my face was changing again. He wanted to know the name of whatever men she was dealing with. All mama kept yelling out to him was that he was the only man. She kept asking him why he felt it was his responsibility to try and put her down every chance he got. She always started off strong during their debates. It was her middle and end that she'd end up whimpering. It was a bad pattern. I told her that. I told her to get it together and walk out. I told her ain't nothing more painful than feeling trapped. I told her their union was more like torture and that one day she'd see what they really have but by then it would be too late," said Mariah.

"I wasn't expecting that. Did she ever really listen to your advice? How did you approach your father? Despite the difficulties do you wish deep down inside that your parents could be together? What about Elaine? What really happened to her? Did you kill her? You left things up in the air about her. It seems like that would be the only reasonable possibility. If you didn't, who did?" asked Rebecca.

"I didn't expect it either, but as things began to unravel, it seemed almost logical. My parents lived their vows based on survival, not love. They both hindered one another from growing, because they were scared to see what life would be like on their own. Neither of them wanted to be married, but marriage was the ideal image that they needed in order to live out their truest desires. It's kind of like they allowed one another to be the scapegoat for their selfish needs and insecurities. It was much more like a bad business deal. So, what happened as time progressed? They died inside with each passing second. I wouldn't wish what they had on my biggest enemy. I thank God minus all the embarrassment that they were finally able to break free from one another. I wish under different circumstances, but whatever works I guess.

Do you think it's honest to cheat with another married person? But you do think it's okay to do whatever makes you happy right? Does that not come with any stipulations or limitations? You have to consider your morals and your significant other right? See, this is where my parents lacked. These ideas were skipped right over. They didn't have a bond, they secretly had a mutual agreement that they never actually even agreed to. Basically, they both did whatever they wanted because they never thought they'd get caught. Except they did get caught. Mama came clean in some instances, without even knowing. My father kept his show going for so long, he forgot what the truth even means. Elaine yes was the big one for me and my sisters. Well mainly for me. My sisters are younger than I am and they didn't have the same relationship I did with our mother nor their aunt. But my Dad is just as much if not more to blame. He has never had regard for anyone but himself. He's got kids that could be my kids and the nerve to have cried the way he did. A whole wolf I tell ya'. That's why I reacted the way I did initially with Elaine because I've never expected much from my daddy…but she and I were pretty close at one point. My mother aged double being so tired from jail and being broken. Do you know before everything came to the light, I saw her beginning to deteriorate? Yes, indeed child I remember walking into this kitchen and she was sitting at the table reading a brochure. I looked at it and told her you and Daddy should take a trip and she broke down. Of course, I was being a jerk but I didn't mean for her to cry. I held her hand, wiped her eyes and told her I knew that she wasn't happy. I remember she picked up her head and she told me you don't just leave, that every marriage is hard. I told her hard yes, *misery no*. She popped me right in my mouth and told me to stay in a child's place. I told her that I was sorry not for what I said, but sorry that she didn't see her worth and that staying with him would either result in her being destroyed, or experiencing a level of pain she couldn't imagine. I told her she wasn't doing him any good either. She cheated too. She was just as guilty. But a child should never suffer. They were both sad. Just sad... My mother was a praying woman. I knew that too, so I made sure to tell her I felt everything that I said to her in my spirit. My daddy told her and showed her in every way possible that he wasn't going to give her what she wanted nor needed, and could you blame him? He couldn't trust her either. Somehow, they both enjoyed their sick game of having cake and eating it too for a while until life went sour...terribly sour. They both took on way too much. I knew then she was just as bad as he was if not even worst. But she was all I had. He never wanted me. After what she did, he couldn't want me. He didn't know how to. So, it was only natural that I take the bulk of my anger out on him, right?" asked Mariah.

"I'm speechless Mariah. You know none of their wrongdoing is any of your fault. But what about Elaine? I'm really curious as to what really happened to her? We're all dying to know. Please do share. Some feel that you blamed her for the majority of events. Some feel that even though you wanted your mama to leave, you think that part of what tore your father away for good was their affair. Do you think she was a homewrecker? Do you think that's where any of your father's infidelity stemmed from?" asked Rebecca.

"Well now that I really couldn't tell you. I believe I said that during my first sitting. I don't know who else was charged with what. I only know specific details in regards to my own circumstances. So, to answer your question, I was proven not guilty. Not I sugar. Not quite clear who, but damn sure not I. She was having an affair with my dad, there's not much to feel for her. I know it sounds like a contradiction. You're thinking how I can be so angry about my Dad's actions but defend him or still care when considering Elaine's involvement. I couldn't stand her once I learned of their other relationship but I didn't want her dead. I just didn't want her living with my family either. She and my father weren't out in the open prior to mama going away so I felt it was distasteful. But again, I've never wished anything on her. I'm still not one hundred percent clear on all the facts but I was informed not to speak on her passing without my lawyer. As far as her as a person or my aunt…of course I feel like she double crossed me and the whole family. But, I'm a fair woman. It's been years now. I know how to admit when I'm wrong. I strongly disliked her when it all came out. I felt like I knew her better than that. My feelings were biased because she was my aunt and I loved her for my entire life before knowing the truth. She let me down big time. But, as I worked on myself and my healing, I took back a lot of what I said. I know I said a lot! There is no such thing as a homewrecker. I know that now. I probably knew then too but I was furious. A stable house can't be shaken up. So, if someone is able to come on in and start tossing things around in the home you and your significant other built...that bad boy was already on its last leg. Most likely it stopped being a home a long time ago with or without that person you're looking to place the blame on. If she were just a random woman, I would understand that she didn't owe me nor my family anything. I expected different because of her relation but that still didn't take away from my parent's lack of communication and respect for one another. It was an issue in our home, not an issue with my aunt," said Mariah.

"I agree. I think you made a great point in your explanation of outside partners. We're always so quick to jump down a woman who in most cases we rarely know anything about. I think in your case she was wrong as well. But you're right if it were someone else your mother should have still gone to your father. And you as well in your case. Well, can you tell me a little more about the stairs? How did you guys get there? What did she want? Could you give a little more information about Joey? I feel like something isn't adding up," said Rebecca.

"You can't add what you don't have honey. I know you heard me the first time. The stairs involve Elaine's death which means I'm unable to reference anything specific. And I already told you Joey was a good man. He was soft, gentle, and understanding. I was his rock. I pushed him to do and be someone he would have never been. I was the girl on the wrong side of the tracks trying to break free, and he was the one looking to save me. Only we ended up saving each other if that makes any sense. Joey was my lawyer, but before any of that, he was my friend. I believe that's why we connected the way that we did. It was way more than just a physical attraction. I could ask for anything in the entire world, and he would make it his business to make it happen. He made no excuses, if I wanted it, I got it. Aside from my grandfather, Joey was my first experience of what a great man looked like. Did we have tough times? Of course, we did I told you nothing has ever been perfect for me. Have we ever argued? Of course, I have a mouth like a sailor and I stopped being a yes woman years ago. I wanted Joey to have the same spunk he demonstrated in the court room, at home with me. I get it, when you're in love with someone you establish this sort of tenderness for them, but just once in a blue I wanted him to be more daring. What I complained about, most women dreamed. Isn't it hilarious? Women crave for emotion, consideration, and a gentler side… While I wanted more backbone. Nevertheless, I'm not complaining, nor was I then. I didn't want a yes man, that's all. Look at that, I told you we didn't get to be together as long as I wished for yet you still managed to squeeze out some of my fondest and vulnerable moments shared with him," said Mariah.

"Ah, I see. Thank you for attempting to elaborate, however that's still not really answering my question. Could there have been any other cause for Joey's death?" asked Rebecca. "I'm afraid I don't understand where you're trying to go with this. You read the reports, right? So, what other cause would you be assuming Ms. Townsend?" asked Mariah.

"That's correct, I did. Actually, I did multiple times which is why I'm still having difficulties with some of your reasoning. You know it's only my job to report the news. I give people facts, everything that they need and want to know, and for the most part I never ever include my ideas or interpretation. Not only is it not needed, but it's not wanted and it may or may not be true. However, I'm one to follow gut instinct, and I firmly believe that something just isn't making sense here. Let me explain, your parents traumatized you. This is a fact. Your grandmother and your aunt on your father's side never accepted you due to circumstances you had no way of controlling. Your mother's sister the almost famous Elaine created more injury as one of your father's many mistresses, and now the one man you trusted the most magically up and died? Oh, and I forgot on top of his recent death you seem to be just fine," said Rebecca.

"Well child you're right you damn sure are the boss. That was a wonderful break down. But again, what are you getting at aside from the fact that I don't care to broadcast my tears? Like you just said I've had a few bumps so all of that only shows that I've learned how to control my losses. Is there a crime in holding back? Am I breaking some sort of law by not sitting here with multiple boxes of tissues? We all mourn differently you know," asked Mariah?

"I guess so, it just seems odd. Sort of like these visuals that were taken just days before his passing," said Rebecca.

Rebecca opens up her brief case and pulls out an envelope marked Mariah Scandal on it in scripted letters. She sits up on the couch, takes a sip from her water that Mariah offered when they first began, and hands her the envelope to hold as she places each image on the coffee table. She explains that a good journalist takes risks to get the story and how she knew that there is much more going on than what Mariah was willingly sharing about Joey. She said she didn't buy his death pitch, that it seems strange, and awkward. Mariah looks really pale, but she still manages to keep a grin on her face. She watches Rebecca rejoice while telling how she followed her and a mysterious man for months before Joey died. She starts getting more and more excited as she recounts moments where she hid behind trees, cars, and even in a closet once just to get the details first. Next, she asked her about an idea that ran through her mind since before they even met. She asked if she was ever involved with Justyce McCall. Mariah's grin instantly turns to a frown. She feels like Rebecca is not only disrespecting her, but Justyce as well. Rebecca noticed the tension and immediately backs up her curiosity. She tells Mariah that she reviewed the first documentary and she saw lots of loop holes.

She said she's viewed other works by Justyce, and never has he been biased before.

"I think it's time for you to go now Rebecca. I'm not a fan of being stalked. What you have here are pictures of myself and a family friend enjoying one another's company. Clearly, I just said every relationship has its ups and downs. Wouldn't you think there's a possibility Joey and I were separated at the time? No, of course the first thing you think is that I stepped out on Joey or even had something to do with his murder. But Justyce is the biased one right," asked Mariah?

"Did you just say murder?" asked Rebecca.

"No, what are you talking about now girl. For one second take your head out of your tail and stop trying to develop your own narrative opposed to the actual facts," said Mariah.

"There's no need to patronize me. I know what I heard, and you know too. Leave your sarcasm where you probably left your fiancé. You're worried about not having the chance to ever get married and you probably stuffed the soon to be one you would have had somewhere in a trunk or a ditch. Child which seems to be your favorite word, I think you're just as messy as your family. I see through the fake soul," said Rebecca. "I beg your pardon you, ingrate. You are totally out of line. It is a privilege for you to be in my presence. You speak to me like this in my own home? You know what not only do I want you to leave, but you can let your so-called organization know the second part is off. I will not speak with anyone who thinks of me the way you do. Keep your camera, keep your exposure, and get out of my house right now! I will not ask you again," yelled Mariah.

"Do you feel the need to raise your voice because I've double-dutched all over your argument? Did I hit a nerve? Or better yet did I touch base on some unsettling truth you've been holding back? Justyce doesn't want to be with you! Honey you're no celebrity, just a sad woman from a sick twisted family. Listen if it were up to me, you'd be finished. I know you're a murderer. How many others have you killed," asked Rebecca?

"If you don't get off of my couch and make your way towards the door, I bet I'll expand my foot! I'm really trying my hardest to spare you. You have no idea who you're dealing with sugar but you're getting ready to find out," said Mariah.

"Let's not make any promises that can't be kept Mariah. All I asked were a few simple questions, and all you did is give me the responses that I need. You are right, maybe you were broken up with Joey during the time of those photos. Maybe they occurred a little sooner than his passing. But, maybe they didn't. Maybe the man pictured is not Justyce who all of a sudden is sick and can't be here with you. Maybe it's a whole different person. Maybe you followed in your father's footsteps. It's possible that you find excitement in multiple relationships than just one occurrence like your mother. Or, have you tried any of your sibling's spouses yet? Is that it? Did you become obsessed with Elaine and decide to follow her lead? Uh oh I think I'm onto something hot now! Is that why you had to kill her as well as Joey? Did they both get in your way? Come on answer me Mariah. What happened? You wanted this platform just a little while ago. Is it too much too handle now? Is the truth no longer going to set you free? Don't you want to be a movie star? What about a book? I can really see your name in lights girl. Huh? What happened I can't hear that voice so loudly anymore. Are you mad you can no longer manipulate the situation and be the fake victim that you pretend to be?" asked Rebecca.

"I believe I asked you more than once to get up and leave. Turn off the camera right now! I'm done recording. You're right Rebecca, you are absolutely right. However, you talk too damn much and you should have taken all of your clues and fled to safety. I tried to be nice, I really did. Like how much nonsense can you expect to blurt out before I retaliate? I don't bother anyone, I never did. Yet here you are in my face trying to make a mockery out of me. Are you familiar with what happens to curious people? Wait I got one better for you. Are you familiar with what happens to brainless people that attempt to disturb my peace!" screamed Mariah.

Mariah stands up and makes her way toward the kitchen. The whole time she's shouting different curse words in Spanish and French. Rebecca begins to panic. Apparently, her notes aren't all that great. She only knew that Mariah is black and white. She has no other background information especially nothing that states she is fluent in other languages. As she finally begins to take heed by packing up her belongings, the wooden kitchen drawer slams and Mariah creeps back toward the living room. Except she looks different. She has on jeans, work boots, and a black T-shirt. Her hair is pulled back in a low ponytail, and she looks like she's on her way out.

"I apologize for the disruption," said Rebecca. You're right, I don't have all of my notes intact, and I shouldn't have presented such until I made sure I was completely ready to do so. It's magnificent that you speak other languages. I haven't read that anywhere before. You're Hispanic? And do you have a closet somewhere in your kitchen? I've never seen someone get dressed as quickly as you did. I heard things still moving around, so I didn't know if you stepped out to go into your bedroom. But again, you are absolutely right. I've been out of line the entire time. I'm a professional but I wasn't conducting myself as such so I'll gather myself and make my way back toward the office. This isn't me. I'm sorry for getting so worked up. I'm not one to judge," said Rebecca.

"You're fine, child...besides what's done is done right? It's just a little too late. I thought you were here for the same reasons as Justyce, but I see now that I am wrong and Justyce is right. I also asked you nicely to get up and go but you chose to play a game that you're not trained for. Your facts aren't so far off. You're getting pretty close. But you should have waited before sharing. Your premature bust will cost you a lot," said Mariah.

"What game? I'm not playing any sort of game Mariah. I'm woman enough to admit to my mistake. I can see that I'm wrong. What is Justyce right about? You know what, it doesn't even matter. I should just respect your wishes and do as asked. How about I head on out. We can eliminate my notes and whenever Justyce returns, you all can pick up where you left off. Honestly, I think that's the best idea. Like you said you don't like change, and you began with him, so wouldn't you like to end with him?" asked Rebecca.

"That's right, that's what I said then, but this is now. And what if Justyce and I already did end," asked Mariah. "I'm not quite sure that I'm understanding you, what do you mean?" asked Rebecca. "What if Justyce doesn't have the flu Rebecca? Come on you're a smart woman don't play stupid now. You had it all just a minute ago. What would you assume happened to him? I mean you said he never calls out, where else could he be? What else could he be doing?" asked Mariah.

"What are you implying Mariah," asked Rebecca. "You claim you know him so well. I'm not implying anything. One thing you should know, I don't play. If I'm bringing something up, it's because it is relevant and you should probably pay very close attention. Well you should have, can't really help you now," said Mariah.

"It's really never too late for anything. Look I don't know anything more than I'm told. This means you don't have to say another word and I can just walk away. I honestly just wanted to cover the bulk of your story because it's a mystery we've all been inquiring about. We don't get too much excitement down here. It's been an ongoing story. It's 2015 now like how cool would it be to solve Elaine's murder? But I get it. I totally get it. If you'd like Justyce or whoever else, I'm completely fine with that. I think we got off to a bad start and my intense poking for clues rubbed you the wrong way. I didn't mean to come off like a groupie. Again, I'm a journalist and it's made me a bit of an investigator as well. But, I'm no fool. This is beyond my expertise so I'll just be on my way. All of my things are ready. I just have to find where I put my keys. I know I had them in my hand when I sat down," said Rebecca.

"You mean these keys right here," said Mariah. "You have to be careful where you leave your stuff. That's how things get misplaced."

"Oh, thank you for finding them. That's true, silly of me I normally place them in my coat pocket I guess I didn't even notice," replied Rebecca.

"Yeah that's it, you didn't notice. You don't notice a lot of things Rebecca. That's not good, you should open your eyes up. Justyce caught on much quicker if I do say so myself," said Mariah. "Justyce caught onto what Mariah? What am I missing now," asked Rebecca. "Moment of truth, I knew who you were the moment I opened the door. If you studied my first interview, you'd know I do my research too. Like I really knew who you were, not just based upon the company you work for. I'm not the only one that has an eye for Justyce am I? Think about it, one of your first thoughts was whether or not he handled our conversation in a professional manner, right? Well go head speak up girl... don't be shy now", said Mariah.

"Yes, Justyce and I once discussed a relationship outside of the work place, but it didn't go anywhere. We both decided that our careers are more important and that we work well and that's it," said Rebecca.
"Bravo, bravo that was almost believable. Give me a break you simple minded broad. I can read you. I can look into your eyes and see that if Justyce gave you the time of day, you'd do everything in your power to tickle his fancy," said Mariah.
"No Mariah you're wrong. I'm not interested in Justyce at all. Is there something between you two? Is that what you're trying to unveil? Because I

promise you, he's not worth my time nor any type of discrepancy with you. You have my word I have no relations with him nor have I ever," said Rebecca. "Are you sure? Did he ever tell you I really hate being lied to? If he didn't, I know I did, so why are you lying girl? Plus, my photographer seems to have much better angles than yours," said Mariah. "I'm lost, what are you talking about," asked Rebecca?

Mariah pulls a package of her own from behind her back and tells Rebecca to open it. Inside are pictures of Rebecca and Justyce. Rebecca tries to explain but Mariah waves a knife and tells her to quit it.

"Save it child. If my eyes aren't mistaken, these here images look like a little more than editing revisions to me. It looks like you're trying to create more than just an article. It looks more like a movie if you ask me. Look at how passionate you are. Oh, how romantic,' said Mariah.

"You have no Business…"

"Oh, you mean like the business you thought you had in following me," said Mariah. "I was just doing my job. What is your excuse?" said Rebecca. "Sweetie take that bull elsewhere. You took on this story because you think Justyce and I are a thing and that bothers you because you want you and Justyce to be a thing. But from the looks of the pictures you all are a thing only in your mind. Can't you see he's using you," asked Mariah.

Rebecca begins to lose her cool. She tries to get up but Mariah shoves her back onto the couch. She balls her fist and swings; however, she misses. Mariah scoops her up with one arm and carries her towards her room. She has two closets, one filled with clothing, and the other that's absolutely empty. She bangs Rebecca's head against the wall as she tosses her into the empty closest and whispers "Don't worry your wish is my command. I promise to make it quick and painless just as I did with Justyce. I promise you two can finally be together just as you wanted." Rebecca tries to lift herself up but she can't. She's suffering from a concussion, and her arms and legs feel so numb. She barely can see, it's so dark and cold. Mariah leaves out the room and turns on the radio. Rebecca tries her hardest to wake up. Finally, she pulls out some strength and gains feeling back in her body. She starts to kick at the door but it won't budge. She begins yelling and crying but nothing changes. The music only gets louder and louder and she can hear Mariah's mischievous laugh as if she were still right next to her. She refuses to give up, her kicks become more frequent and soon she is able to stand up straight in attempt to grab the door knob. That's when she feels something almost directly behind her. She lets out a huge screech and that's when Mariah's laugh comes closer again. Mariah opens the door cracking up and says "Well I thought I was giving you what you wanted." There he is, Justyce McCall's lifeless body. Rebecca tries to get up, but there's no way. She was knocked out for a much longer period than she thought. While in the closet, Mariah gave her a shot in both her arms. That explained the numbness for some time. She's still trying to be strong and fight against Mariah but she can't. "Why are you doing this," asked Rebecca. "What did we do to you?" "Why am I doing this? Oh gosh, spare me, you big cry baby. Why would I not do this? Do you know what I've been through? Do you know that you both contributed and are just as guilty? Like I said, your angles are slightly off but you're dumb mind is surely dead on. I was indeed seeing someone during the time of Joey's death. And I believe even without seeing his face you know exactly who it was," said Mariah.

Rebecca looks at Mariah with a look of confusion. Then she looks at Justyce McCall's body. On his wrist she sees the initials MSB. She starts to think about a past conversation she had with Justyce while drinking coffee at a local diner one day last year. She saw the initials and she asked him what they stood for. At the time he said they belonged to his mother and that her name was Marian Sara Brixton. She said to him well where does McCall come from and he said his parents were never married. Mariah starts to laugh because she knows he told her that lie. She then pulls out a picture of Lillian and Johnathan McCall and hands it to Rebecca. As soon as she fixes her mouth to object, the picture right behind it has Justyce right in between them and a written caption that says "To the best parents ever…I love you." Rebecca doesn't know what to say. She tries to stop the tears, but she knows she can't. She knew her intuition was spot on but now there isn't anything she can really do. She assumes Mariah handled things the best way she saw fit.

"So, you've exposed Justyce for the cheater that he was. I guess it's safe to say you killed him, right? So now what? What do you want from me? What are you expecting from this," asked Rebecca?

"I did what? What do you mean? I got home and found you and Justyce both in my closet. I saw that you used some sort of drug or something to give you a high and ultimately killed him after finding out that he had relations with someone else. His tattoo dedicated to whomever he was dealing with just so happens to have the same initials as me," said Mariah. "You cannot be serious. Are you kidding me? This has all spun way out of control. Okay I am wrong. I wanted to know the truth about Justyce so I used you. But we both know I'm not the blame for this. In fact. I would never," said Rebecca.

"Oh. never say never babe. That's not what your little letter says." "What letter are you talking about? I didn't write anything and you know it. Wait a minute are you trying to frame me for something else? What did or didn't Justyce do for you?" asked Rebecca. "AH HA, now you're getting somewhere my girl. Justyce chose to go in a different direction from what we had planned. If it weren't for you, he would have ruined everything that I worked so hard for," said Mariah.

"But how exactly do I help? I swear to you I don't know anything about anything you all had going on. All I knew was that he wasn't just working on your story. He was fixated on you and I knew deep down it was more than just your timeline of tragic events that stole his interest," said Rebecca.

"You help because you have a motive my dear jealous witch. You basically just said it. You knew we had something going on. Although you still don't know nearly what you should, your heated rage brought you here where you thought you'd catch us both in the act. You were wrong but your pride couldn't stand it. So, you killed Justyce and like a weakling you ended your life as well," said Mariah "Wait a minute, I ended my life as well? I wouldn't hurt anyone and I damn sure would never inflict pain on myself." "Yeah, Yeah... I figured you wouldn't so that's why I'm here to help. Duh, what are killers for?" asked Mariah.

Rebecca tries to get up and make a run for it, but the drugs are still holding her hostage. Mariah starts laughing like a maniac again before firing three shots. One hit Rebecca's arm, the other hit her leg, and the final shot hit right in the middle of her forehead. Rebecca's eyes tear as she tries to make one last statement but the impact won't allow it. But she won't just give in, she pushes hard before falling directly in front of Justyce McCall.

"Well that sure took longer than planned. Is it safe to move now? Is she dead?" asked Justyce. "If you listened to me in the first place this wouldn't have happened. I don't even know what you saw in her. Look, she practically begged. She didn't even put up an award-winning fight. I'm telling you now Justyce something like this better not ever happen again. You really almost ruined everything. How long do you think before XYZ-8 will be calling? Did you even think that far? No don't answer. Don't even lie. All you thought of was yourself. Good job, it's because of you another one bites the dust." said Mariah.

"Oh, so now everything is my fault? What about you Mariah. I have been telling you for weeks already that she was constantly asking me about you and I. That's why we had no choice. I told you she was going to pull some kind of stunt sooner or later. And look the first chance she got, she came looking for you. Now my problem is out of the way but how about yours. Really cremation? I almost laughed out loud literally. I've been telling you just as long about Joey. If everyone already thinks he is dead, why isn't he? The money has cleared, what is the hold up? Still some lingering feelings?" asked Justyce.

"It's the first thing that came to my mind. The world knows the edited story about what happened to Joey. Your little girlfriend was the first person to question me and the actual cause of death. I didn't know if she was going to ask more about his body. Plus, Joey hasn't been and isn't an issue. He is hipped to the original plan. You know the one where the money just cleared from his life insurance plan, and he and I running off to Cuba. I don't think I ever gave him the second draft that includes me and the man that's supposed to be writing about me having an affair, and planning his murder for real. Also. he's very much clueless. He doesn't suspect anything between you and me. He thinks that you believe that he's already dead too. All he knows is that we have the continuation of the series tomorrow, and by the end of the week we'll be living the life. See unlike you I run my show and any show that I'm a part of. But you will see," said Mariah.

CHAPTER ONE
Justyce, Where Did We Leave Off

The leaves have changed colors at least three times. No need for a sweater, it won't help. With this strong wind, you'll need a heavier coat for sure. You probably could use a hat and a pair of gloves too. I haven't worn a heel in quite some time. I've grown to love sneakers and flat shoes. For this weather, they're definitely the better choice anyway. My left hand is swollen, the cold chapped my lips, and my hair hasn't been touched in weeks. Hell, it's always in a bun anyway. I try not to go out too much especially when the weather is this bad. In most cases, I'm at the store and right back. I don't even like checking the mail anymore to be honest. My home phone rings nonstop and one would wonder how being that I don't have associates let alone friends. But, for the right price a relative or two won't mind sliding it through the cracks. I've learned a pretty penny goes further than loyalty for far more people than you'd think. Of course, I learned that long ago but thought just maybe things had changed a little…guess not. Today is the day everyone has been waiting for. It's April 13th, 2015 and Justyce and I are going to sit down for round two. We were supposed to meet yesterday but we were both a little tied up so we rescheduled for today.

They're bringing up the past again... can you believe it? Just as the seasons continue to change, why can't I? Why can't they just leave me alone already? It's like they saw that they couldn't get me for what they originally wanted, so now they're trying a new route. Let go and let God already. It's becoming more and more pathetic with each passing day. What good is focusing on something that can't be changed? Why are they still trying to develop nonexistent facts and witnesses? Blah blah blah, Mariah this and Mariah that. That's all I ever hear. Meanwhile, I'm just trying to mind my business and live the best life that I possibly can despite the traumatic hand I was dealt and their terrible interpretation of my character. People I've never even met before have some of the most profound opinions about events they weren't around for. On top of that, they have so much false information about me it's ridiculous. Theories from every which way. The latest came out last week. A woman says it's a conspiracy the way in which my case and everything following has managed to go on without a real punishment for so many years. This same lady should be thanking me. Do you know her husband emailed my lawyer inquiring about lunch? Yea, I guess he didn't realize Joey was more than just business. He also didn't realize he was still married. Focused on me, look what happens! Then, the twins called maybe two days ago. They said a man came by both their homes asking about me too. He said he was writing something for a series he's working on. The first thing he asked them was if I was a teen mother, and what disturbing facts could they give him. I can't help but to laugh and ask which news station or magazine put him up to it. I saw in another local newspaper a few days ago that they believe they may have found a new lead? Ha, that's the same thing they said last year and you want to know what happened? That lead played a dirty game with a corrupt cop and they're both now serving time. If that's not irony I don't know what is. Want to know something else about that so-called lead?

She's related to me, yup my cousin to be exact. And what about the dirty cop right? He and Joey played little league together. Joey made a few files disappear from him a decade ago. During this setup, they magically resurfaced and well that was that. You could write a novel on all of this I tell you, just something else. But, I'm rather intrigued to know who and how this new person came about. Who has the time to keep chasing a dead story? I better choose my words wisely, dead might insinuate a possible confession. Most people are still so touchy and take whatever I say literally. That's what they want most, they want me to agree to something that isn't true. I got off and that's that! I defeated the curse because I dropped the façade, learned to love myself and everything that comes with me. This means I dropped my pride and learned from my family's generational imperfections and secretive ways. I did what they couldn't. That should be the end of the story. I lived up to my part in this whole ordeal. I also spent time in the hospital, I do believe that counts for something. I'm just sick of it! My Aunt's devastating death came as a shocker to us all. I wish she could be here today but she's not. How long am I supposed to be down in the dumps, or at least pretend to be? Am I not supposed to move on?

Dr. Blue and I spoke about everything. Before letting him into my way of viewing family and relationships, I asked that he let me council him. I wasn't too sure what the answer would be, but he actually agreed. I guess it was a tactic to show that he was really my friend. I was never convinced, but I was receptive to playing with him. Fun fact, he became a doctor to help others prevent their minds from enduring the destruction that his has. That was deep, so of course I couldn't just leave it as that. He didn't want to share specific details, I think he realized I'd swindled my way along lines that no one else had before. Most times I would lay on his turquoise sofa placed right by his tawny colored desk and have my way assessing his every movement for at least an hour. Observations were key, like around his room which was bright with at least six shades of blue, lots of wood, and glass…only had about four pictures and they were old. Where was his family? Why doesn't he have his kids and wife hanging up? Well, after a few glasses of wine and some exhaling activities, he gave me everything I needed. He was originally from Brooklyn New York. He left the state after a horrific accident that costs him his wife and two young sons. He was going to break things off with his wife because he was seeing another woman. I wanted to give him the illusion that he couldn't be a cheater but my goodness he was hotter than a night in Savannah Georgia. He's not pure, a mix of Black and Irish. His hairs dirty blonde, light green eyes, taller than two of me stacked on top of each other, built like a Greek God woo wee I could go on forever.

But anyway, the woman he had an affair with was one of his patients. I know, isn't that something the Doctor trying to prevent yucky occurrences actually lived through one. I know honey I know. Anyway, He called his wife whom he called sweet Gwendolyn, and told her they needed to speak. The day before he called his mistress who he referred to as Temper, and told her he'd no longer like to handle her case. He explained that he really wanted her to get well, but that their relationship was not helping her in the way she really needed to benefit. Temper saw darkness... she realized his heart belonged to his family. Her solution was to hurt them as an attempt to break him. So, she started following his wife and accidentally banged into her car one day right in front of his office. Now, do you file against the crazy patient you've been having rendezvous with or do you help her plead insanity and walk away with nothing but your job still? Yes, Dr. Blue chose his job. After releasing such information, I could tell he felt a sense of relief. But how exactly would he go about handling things with me? He wasn't sure, so I told him. I gave him a list of questions to ask me. I told him when we'd meet, how to pay attention to my gestures, what my triggers were, and how to bring me back to a place of peace. I told him how

I'd interject, and try to avoid certain memories. I told him how to doctor me. I told him not to back off until I answered his questions, and expressed my feelings at all times. Ultimately, I guided him into letting me free way before I should have and in return, I closed my eyes to his secret life. Honestly, it wasn't my business. I really went digging for that, and I didn't think he'd really fall for it. But that's what happens when people haven't let things go, with the right touch they can still appear. I must admit playing reverse doctor on him really introduced me to a calmer way of coping with issues. But since I now knew he was just like those that hurt me. I decided not to let him in my thoughts. That's when I switched to Dr. Pressleigh. My family would have never discussed our business with an outsider even if forced to. I could see daddy now he'd probably just look away. And mama, she'd smile and decline at the same time. As for everyone else, it wouldn't be debatable. No matter which Dr. I chose for whatever reason, they just weren't that open. I still don't get it. This is as sensitive of a topic for me as it is for anyone else. I didn't kill Elaine. *Jealousy killed Elaine.* I loved her then and even today I still love her. Even after the confusion, the betrayal, the blatant disrespect, I loved her. I know now that she just suffered from the curse and unfortunately, she wasn't able to break free. But, no one deserves to die, especially the way that she did. Nevertheless…

My testimony remains the same! I'm not guilty of anything... not then and definitely not now! It was ruled an accident, and that's what it was. I was angry and hurt, not crazy and violent. It's like everyone is waiting for a reaction, some sort of psychotic lashing out. However, nothing has changed in my behavior, or my story. It was a bit of a tussle, nothing too serious. She grabbed me, pulled my hair to one side. That I do remember. I shoved her, I tried my best to dodge her blows. She came right back squeezing me by the wrist. She really wanted to strike me real hard. I kicked her with all my might, and she fell to the ground.

And after that…as I keep saying, I really can't say. But what does it even matter? Like what do I need to do to prove my innocence again for the second time? Whatever happened once I blacked out is neither here or there, because in the eye of the law, I'm free. I said it, I'm a free woman. So, why is any of this still a topic of discussion?

Dr. Pressleigh says it's important to discuss our past, and what and who created it. Or did I tell him that during his break down? I'm not too certain to tell you the truth. I reversed roles on him for a brief moment too but his pain stemmed from losing his mother to breast cancer. She was all he had. Anyway, a lot of events led up to the brutal altercation that day in the house. My world was basically turned upside down and everything and every person that I knew, I realized I hadn't the slightest clue as to who or what they really were. I read multiple letters, I pieced together most of the puzzle, yet still I felt like there were some things that just weren't out in the open. Aunt Elaine still didn't seem like she had enough reason to go about things the way she did. I mean Daddy was just as accountable, but he and mama were a whole other story. Two days before Aunt Elaine tragically fell, I went to her home. No, not my home that she so rightfully tried to claim as her own, but her actual residence. You know, 120 Heaven Leigh Road. I went there to check things out of course. I dragged her clothes through the mud, I mean I really made a mess. Some of the hideous pieces still had tags on them.

I lifted the mattress, removed the silky fuchsia sheets, cut through the plush pillows, and accidentally dropped the vanity mirror. Shouldn't be so vain if you ask me. I pulled out every drawer in the dresser. I removed each article of clothing, and it wasn't until I dug into the last one that I finally found something. I opened it up all the way. I felt so defiant, secretly I was excited. I wrapped it back up, and put it in my pocket. I knew she'd lose it, and I knew she would figure that it had to have been me. That's why she was so enraged during our encounter. But she couldn't come straight out and say it, I mean who would want to admit to what she did. She wanted to tighten her hands around my neck. She wanted to pull life right up from under me. But she couldn't without getting back what I stole. Plus, if the rest of the family found out, she would have been ruined. Honestly, she was fairly intelligent that I can never take from her. I planned to inform everyone, but not as soon as she thought. She could have stalled and thought her process or attack rather out a little better. She died trying to prevent mama from knowing that they had much more in common than she knew...

My fiancé is nothing more than a devastating coincidence. Oh Joey, he was such a great man. He would literally do anything for me. I didn't even have to ask. I remember growing up watching the women around me in verbally and mentally abusive relationships. It was like a never-ending cycle. Once they thought they found a good one, they would tell him about their other relationships and it was as if that was the green light to follow up with the same behavior. It was like something clicked in them and all of a sudden, the fairy tale faded. I followed their footsteps begging guys and Daddy as well. I didn't learn until I met Joey. He made me so happy. He made me so proud, he really wasn't like any other guy. He wanted me for me and only me. He was interested in everything that I did, everything I said, and he wanted to be involved, whether good or bad. Secrets that I told no one, not even Melody and Melissa, I shared with him. He listened, he responded, but there was never any judgment. I admired that, I appreciated him. He stood by my side the entire trial. He was more than my lawyer, and lover. He was my best friend. So young, so ambitious... however accidents happen. You know that as well as I do. I hope I'm not coming off heartless. Yes, I was hurt. I'm still hurting now, but life goes on. I have to keep moving forward. He would want me to continue with our plans. After the trial we talked about getting married and traveling as primary forms of income. Anywhere the sun shined him and I were sure to go. Talk about a ride or die…literally. Alright that might have been a bit of sick humor. Come on, lighten up. Don't give me that look Justyce. Sometimes you have to laugh, it's the only way to keep from crying. But I loved Joey, I still love Joey. I always have, and I always will.

That's why it's okay for me to joke like this, it's encourages my progress. Although not well, you do know me a little better now Justyce so I feel like you should be aware of and understand my sick sense of humor by now. I work best through negatives, you know pain, misery, grief, so it's only fair to find a bright side when I can. You can't take me too serious though. Actually, you can't take anything too seriously hell that's how we ended up where we are right? I say all of this to say NO one will ever understand the bond Joey and I shared, and what we did for one another. The sacrifices we made, and the reasons why. Just as much as he gave me my second chance, I gave him his. I showed him what it meant to live life freely without having to constantly drain his mind on the ideas of others. I encouraged him to go out there and get it. No, I really encouraged him to take it, and I mean that in the cockiest way. After my case, he knew he had the ability to do anything he put his mind to. But he also learned that he was so much more than just his occupation title. His job was what was expected of him. Our time together was what he was deprived of. No one else could have given him what I gave him. Did we do things that we shouldn't have? ABSOLUTELY! Did I manipulate him here and there? Did I set a bad example? Well, I introduced him to the Mariah he needed to see. We've known each other for years, but it wasn't always on the level that it was right before the accident. Joey was the closest thing I ever had to a real companion. I'll have that in my heart forever. I regret that he was taken too soon before wowing the rest of you like he was wowing me. He was really going to be something special you know? I'm thankful and blessed to have even but a few magical memories with him. I'm more than sure that I was too much for him at times, but he never complained. I mean opposites attract, but we were really like day and night. I'm still devastated, but somehow, I feel like it was in his favor for things to end the way they did you know? There goes another startled look. I don't mean anything by it. I just have a way with getting my way and Joey had an infatuation with helping me keep it that way. But sometimes it was too much. He could never stand up to me.

Do you think I'm scary Justyce? Could you stand up to someone like me? Don't answer that. That's probably the one thing I didn't find attractive at all. Out of respect, I made sure he never knew. But I wished he were verbally stronger. I wish he spoke his mind and went with just his thoughts at times because in some instances he made the most sense. He was just too much of a coward to take control of things.

It's like his spirit was almost too pure and well that was a turn off from time to time. Even when I tried to tell him how to fix it, he'd still backtrack. I had no choice but to step out on our relationship. I needed thrill, I needed to feel like a woman, and I needed someone to dominate, I needed to live. I never let it slip, I wouldn't let it slip. When I first came home from the hospital, I believe the second day, we began receiving phone calls at the house. He didn't know how to handle it. He didn't know what to do. He said he didn't want things to conflict with his career and all I remember saying to myself is what a punk! Pick up the phone, show them who the boss is. You're good at your craft, you can go anywhere. Don't allow anyone to disrespect you or your home. But no, Joey did everything by the book. Well, for the most part. He would pick up the phone and kindly ask that whoever is on the receiving end please stop harassing him and disturbing his home. We didn't always agree either, but some days I do still miss him and wish he was here with me. It was a horrific accident…

I'll never fully get over it.

I've taken many losses, but the greatest gain was Karma. You're probably thinking who in their right mind would be excited about Karma as it holds a nasty taste in most people's mouths, however Karma is my sister. No really, I found out my dad has more children than the siblings I was already aware of. Talk about a surprise. I'm just kidding, I'm not the least bit surprised. He had an affair with a woman named Avah while away on business in Peru. When she told him, she was expecting he told her he wanted nothing to do with either of them. She knew she made a mistake indulging with a married man so she named the little girl Karma as both of their reminder of what they did. Of course, Daddy didn't pay that any mind though…

She's only two years younger than the twins and Mama still has no clue. You know they say after serving time, you're never quite the same. Sometimes you grow and in other cases you lose yourself. I'm not sure where mama falls in, but I don't think she grew too much.

Anyway, Karma really is something else. We're so much alike it's pretty terrifying. Our greatest similarity, is our need for acceptance rather respect. She also likes taking matters into her own hands just as I do. Let's just say she doesn't tolerate any junk and the last thing you'd ever want to do is cross her. It's funny the way the world works. I never would have thought I'd have a sister from Peru or that we would ever meet. She's an investigator too. Not an actual one, you know sort of like me. Her mother Avah Garcia and her stepfather who raised her as his own, Adam Garcia never wanted her to find Daddy. Just six months after she was born, her mother met Adam. They dated for a year and were married. Avah told Adam about the way Daddy felt and he chose to step up to the plate. He has been the only father she knows since then. But, Karma always had a feeling that something just wasn't right. Her siblings all look like her mother, and she doesn't look like her nor like Adam. I mean she has her mother's white complexion, but that's about it. The rest of her features are identical to daddy. She discovered this once she tore the house upside down looking for a copy of her birth certificate. She found a picture of him. She knew her mother must have taken it. He was dressed for a date or some sort of special engagement. The moment she saw the picture she knew he was her Dad or somehow related to her. She just didn't know how to go about proving it. She wasn't sure when exactly would be an appropriate time to mention it. She figured it out though, I'll tell you more about it in due time. I wouldn't want to spoil things so soon. Child if you thought our discussion before was something, you haven't seen anything just yet.

Well, another day another case. I would say I'm blindsided but I'm actually not. It's life, well at least mine anyway. Plus, I've escaped the good old Silent Curse once, I don't scare easily. We're back at the drawing board…Before I start, I have a few demands once again. Not anything out of the ordinary. I want viewers to walk away shattered. I want them to think the unthinkable and feel the impossible. Justyce this has to be your greatest production. I know we all applaud part one but the feedback I expect from this continuation should make it seem miniscule. Not to be arrogant, but that's how important this is to me. Please make sure that I finish all of my thoughts before following up with another question. I know you were great about this last time but I've had a few quarrels in between our last visit. Don't ask me anything about NEWZ-22 either. I dated the anchor for a whole six months back in junior high. It didn't end well. He never got over the break up. We're way beyond grown and he recently got in contact with my manager inquiring about a date. I said maybe, but only as a friend. He sort of found out about Joey.

I mean Joey wasn't supposed to exist as my significant other according to him, so I guess you could say I was in the wrong. Oh well, you win some and you lose some right? With that being said most of their coverage is biased because of our history. I wasn't aware until much later, but he wanted marriage, and I wanted fun. I was with Joey. I thought he'd help with growing my exposure. Not being equally yoked, and lack of communication stopped that joy ride rather quickly. Like how do you tell someone that wants to marry you that you're already about to get married? I know poor guy, but you can't make yourself feel something that you don't feel. I didn't think he'd get so attached especially that soon. Also, the documentary has been featured everywhere thanks to you of course. Do we really have to go back to the beginning? Everyone should have viewed the first sitting already. How about I just summarize the end of my case and a synopsis on Joey to bring viewers up to speed as to where we are today. From there you can work your magic in regards to editing and whatever else needs to be done to satisfy your following. As stated earlier, a lot has changed. The twins are still away being mothers and following their dreams and well Karma is currently here. She's become my partner in crime... no pun intended. I'm working on my own goals, my wants and needs every day. Right now, what I want the most, is to move on from all of this. I hope this extended interview reaches a lot of deaf ears that act as if they don't hear my voice echoing on a daily basis trying to drown out their assumptions.

I hope it quiets down the nonqualified want to be judges and lawyers, and gives hope to others. I'll give you a little insight that I haven't given anyone else. I think all of this footage has me ready to step in front of the big screen. That's right, you heard it here first. I think acting would suit me, don't you? No need to answer right now, sorry for going off into next field. But I think that's my next direction. So, if you're fine with my request, and there are no current questions, I think I'm ready to begin."

"Wow, you mean I'm in the presence of an aspiring actress? Listen you've already freely opened up to us all so I think it's a wonderful idea," said Justyce.

"Do you really? You don't think the public may try to crucify me?" asked Mariah.

"You're a free woman Mariah. You were proven innocent in a court of law. You can't allow your fears or the concerns of others to get the best of you. Think about it, look where you are now. It's because you took a chance and started believing in yourself. You didn't know what to expect by allowing viewers into your real life. But look how it all worked out in your favor. Physically you are free, now allow your mind and emotions to grasp onto freedom as well," said Justyce.

"You know something Justyce, you're right according to law I'm a free woman myself, right? Accidents are something we didn't intend to happen right? Years ago, you remember me mentioning how my fiancé taught me about self-love and appreciating myself. We were just young kids, but he was always smart. While in High School, he was taking advanced classes, specifically in law. He always wanted to be a lawyer. He said knowing things that I went through gave him the incentive to help others that may not have the resources to help themselves. When we secretly got back in touch with one another, I would say around the time I met up with Forest, I took the chance in telling him everything and asking if he still believed in helping others. I had no money, but I knew I had to come up with a plan. I couldn't watch Elaine just walk away. I was just as mad at Daddy, but for some reason he wasn't a factor as much as she was during the timing of my plan. I felt sorry for daddy and peace within my heart knowing that there wasn't anything wrong pertaining to me. He just couldn't fully love me because he didn't really love himself. I realized that hurt people hurt people. He also didn't know his worth, and she tricked him just like everything else. He was just her way of getting to Mama and she was his in return. I felt no animosity towards him for I knew guilt would kill him in a way that actual death never could.

I wasn't sure how my fiancé would react, nor if he'd think I was some sort of a circus freak with all of my history. I was desperate, and going to give it a try. Well, to my surprise, he said he wanted to help me. He said the best thing is to face my demons that way I can move forward. I'm thinking oh joy he's implying that I should host some sort of a pow wow with her and cry it out. I was wrong…

He said sometimes you have to take matters into your own hands; you have to take back control of your life. It's not your fault what you come from, but sometimes you can use it to your advantage. I thought I was hearing him right but at the same time thinking no way, a man in his position couldn't be saying what I thought he was saying. But he was, he really was. So, we came up with the plan for Elaine and I to meet right here in this house. Why here? Well because she loved this house, she swore it and everything in it belonged to her, so why not? The catch is she wasn't just meeting with me. That's right, my fiancé was right by my side…

I do know that she and I had words, and we did get physical by the stairs. However, from there I only remember what me and my fiancé discussed in reference to temporary insanity. He knew with my level of turmoil, that I'd make a great candidate. He figured most likely with his expertise I wouldn't do any time, just the facility for a bit (which I did), he'd keep his career, and in due time all would be well (Living like royalty) Does that answer your question sugar?"

"I believe so, and you're sure that you've shared this with no one else other than myself?"

"Justyce, I'm more than sure honey."

"So, what now?" asked Justyce.

"Well now I'm relieved and stress free. All is out for the world to see right? I mean they can take what I've told you any old kind of way, but my story is the actual truth. So, with that being said, I'm going to continue living the best life that I've now been given. I bet it's horrific to know I literally feel like I just started living. But it's better now than, never right? Joey finally showed me why I had to go through certain experiences, and why it's all more than worth it. I've never experienced love, yet alone a love that holds my happiness above all else. Most people won't even put your feelings first even once, yet Joey did it with each and every situation I can think of. He's one person that knew every single thing about me, and didn't try to use it against me."

"And how do you know that he's never used anything against you? Are you feeling a bit skittish? I notice you keep twirling your hair in between your fingers. If we've gone too far or you've said more than intended, just let me know and you're free to stop," said Justyce.

"What are you trying to say Justyce?"

"I'm not saying anything at all. I'm just curious, with all you've gone through time and time again I'm amazed that you'd trust him to the extent that you do, and so quickly as well. I'm shocked that you'd trust anyone. Actually, I'm surprised you'd ever want to recall such events even with someone like myself."

"It does seem eerie; you're only confused because you don't understand. And, how could you? Why would you? Many things won't always seem likely. But, mind your mouth when speaking about Joey and I. Also don't discredit yourself. I'm a sucker for brilliance, and that you possess. If there's ever a need to worry... I'll take care of it, said Mariah."

"I don't mean to overstep my boundaries, nor offend you. I was only pondering what I'm sure many other speculators have as well. I do thank you for choosing to hold this conference with me, and I wish you and Joey much happiness. However, I did notice something that really struck out... the picture on the wall there of you, Melody and Melissa. Who is the little boy sitting next to Melissa? You never mentioned a little cousin or a brother."

"Oh, you're talking about Michael. Michael is family. He's around the same age as my sisters. He'd come throughout the summer sometimes and one particular weekend we went to take pictures and he was with us. Elaine and daddy didn't want him to feel excluded so they told him to join in," said Mariah.

"Oh, how wonderful. Well that was very sweet of them. He looks like a lovely little boy. Thank you for clearing things up...Uh I really just have one more request," said Justyce.

"Request away," replied Mariah.

"I was wondering if you'd mind giving me a full tour of the house. You know it helps to give a more realistic feeling to the documentary side of things. The entire house is rather significant and I'm sure the viewers would eat it up. Also, we've been sitting for quite a while… I'd love to move around and stretch with you for a bit," said Justyce.

"Child how rude of me, you must think I'm city slick for sure with my lack of manners huh. Of course, I'll show you around. I mean it's not much to it, but I guess you're right. I want the greatest response I can possibly gain from our viewers and listeners, and I value your opinion so we won't debate. I see great opportunities ahead for us as a team. Don't you think? Plus, I just told you everything, what I got to hide right?"

"My thoughts exactly, ahhhh before we begin this wonderful tour, you mind if I use your bathroom? Again, sitting for so long I guess I didn't realize I needed to go before now," said Justyce. "Oh sure, it's right there, down the hall to the left. Soon as you are done just come straight up the steps and I'll start with my old room first," replied Mariah.

"That sounds like a plan to me, I'll be right out in a second," said Justyce.

While inside the bathroom, Justyce begins panicking trying to find a way to deliver such a gripping piece without compromising his career at the same time. He knows Mariah basically came clean. Her fingers dripped in her aunt's blood yet she walked freely. She got away with murder and he isn't sure whether or not to dance or to urge someone to do something. He slid down against the gray walls abruptly hitting the floor. He combed his fingers through his hair and started grinding his teeth together. He's officially stuck between a rock and a hard place. Next, he starts to look around and he notices more pictures of Mariah her sisters and the little boy. It seems like he joined in more frequently than she led him to believe. He stands up to get a closer look at one of the pictures, and notices Mariah's medicine cabinet is slightly cracked. He grabs a square of toilet paper and opens it a little further. His attention is immediately drawn to two bottles. As he picks the bottles up, he hears angry footsteps charging, so he hurriedly closes the cabinet, drops the tissue in the toilet, and flushes it. Unfortunately, Mariah knows something is up. She starts pounding on the wooden door. Justyce softly says he would be right there. She yells out asking if he fell in, and starts to twist at the doorknob. Out of a reaction of fear, Justyce actually needs to use the bathroom but there is no way he'd be able to explain why he flushed the toilet more than once.

"Everything okay? What are you nervous or something? Why is the door locked? Come on Justyce, open up. I opened up to you, now it's your turn. Open the freaking door," said Mariah.

That reply surely let Justyce know that everything isn't okay with her. He doesn't know what exactly is in the bottles, but she most likely chose to skip her dose today. The bathroom is so small, and closed in. There's a tiny window that used to open but it looks like it's been boarded up. High-strung yet disgruntled, Justyce tries banging on the window hoping someone would hear him however the only response he receives comes from Mariah.

"Child, why are you screaming? Don't you know no one can hear you? I bet your hands are grabbing at that curly hair of yours right about now. But yes, if you haven't guessed it, the entire house is sound proof. I forgot to mention that while we were filming. You know I give Joey credit for everything…ugh he was such a devoted fiancé. Well, he wanted to make sure that whatever is said in the house stays in the house…you know like anything that could incriminate me. Not that the documentary was, I felt for sure we had a good thing going. But I did notice a change in your mannerisms during certain statements and I knew just like the rest you'd look for a way to directly say I murdered Elaine. Damn you Justyce, I was hoping you'd be different I really was. But no there you go being just like the others having feelings and what not trying to conflict with your purpose as my storyteller. I got off darling, and you went from being understanding to judging me just like everyone else. What's done is done, I told you that and I meant it. Now, it's going to mean the same for you…now open the door damn it! And don't even think about touching that old phone. It doesn't call out, hasn't since Elaine used to use it actually. Come on, you're starting to make me mad and that's not something you really want dear. I'm done toying around, Open the door now or I'll open it for you," yelled Mariah.

"You don't have to do this Mariah. I'm nobody, just a journalist still fresh in the field. I don't know who all or how many others you've had here nor their whereabouts… that's not any of my business anyway. I totally see that you've reconsidered working together and I'm more than happy to get out of your way. We can discontinue our affairs and nothing mentioned between the two of us will ever leave from here. You have my word. I honestly just wanted to give you the best platform available. I didn't believe that you were guilty nor that it wasn't an accident. But I'm no God nor do I plan to play as such. I have no intention of going to the authorities or anyone else for the matter. What happened to Elaine is none of my business. I'm not the one to step in between family members. I swear to you I know to shut up. This story is absolutely outside of the box for me. Would it have enhanced my career? Yes, it would, but I know when to back away from an opportunity that could possibly hurt more than help" said Justyce.

"If it were only that simple. Justyce, Justyce, Justyce... Sweetie you're smarter than that. You can't bull shit a bull shitter my love. My problem isn't you putting out my story; it's you using my words to dig up something that was verbally and literally buried. The way in which I answered your question left minds wide open. But you had to ask again. So worried about Joey and Elaine. I never admitted but of course, you're no idiot. I know you're ready to sing to any and everybody that'll listen to ya with the first chance you get. I don't have that kind of time. And if by some chance, I'm wrong and that's not your motive, I still can't take that kind of risk. Joey lets go, we have another fighter. He's locked himself in. I asked him several times to come out, so I believe he must want you to come in," screamed Mariah. "Joey? Joey is dead Mariah! You said so yourself. I thought you were going through one of your psychotic phases and that's why I let you continue to talk about him for so long. But he died remember? Who are you talking about? Who is there? Joey are you there? Wait a minute, was that another fake story? You helped her become this? Do you guys think you're going to continue getting away with murdering reputable individuals? How many have there been? Where are they? What is wrong with you? You tell this whole traumatic story; you leave people mesmerized by your pain and suffering. We all pity you, and this is what you do to people that are simply doing what you ask for? How do you think you're any better than those that have hurt you?" asked Justyce.

"Hun we both agreed the interview is long over. Why are you still asking questions like you're the one with the rope and rifle in your hands? I'm trying…deeply trying to have some compassion for you otherwise, I'd blow the door off and you with it. You're testing my patience. I don't want you to go like that. But since you must know everything, the others haven't gone any further than you will," said Mariah.

"What do you mean?" asked Justyce.

"Move the rug from under your feet and you'll see just what I mean," said Mariah. As the rug slowly slid, a shot rang off, the knob dropped, and the door flew open. Justyce fell backwards banging his head on the sink and Mariah and Joey calmly grabbed him by his wrist and ankles. All of Justyce's stuff was all over the toilet and sink. It seemed that although he was trying to find a way out, he knew it was almost impossible. After they drag his body down three flights of stairs,

Mariah returns back to the room to grab his briefcase. She starts laughing hysterically as she cleans and searches through his coat and camera bag…that is until she comes across his wallet and finds two forms of identification. The first says Justyce McCall and the second says Justyce Beauvoir. Mariah nearly dies first realizing that he is a possible relative, and secondly, she questions how exactly are they related because Justyce is younger than she is. Then her mind goes nuts.

"What's wrong, why are you looking at him like that? What else did he do? Did the phone work or something, what am I missing?" asked Joey. "He's not who I think he is. I studied him for so long. I thought just about as long as he probably studied me, but I guess I was wrong. I checked his wallet and his last name is…"

"*No No No No No No*! Are you playing with me right now? You can't be serious, but how? Where is he from? How? Who sent him? You don't recognize him at all? He's younger, how can this be," replied Joey.

Sweat starts to roll down Joey's sunburned face. He begins to unbutton his t-shirt and unzip his jeans which cover a pair of shorts. Then, he tosses them across the side of the tub. Next, he opens up his sweaty palms and places them on his head. Mariah stands there silent, but not Joey.

He is a firm believer that the more people know about them especially in regards to their real story, the tougher things can become for him in regards to his career. He tells Mariah to get undressed as well. He starts talking things through to himself loudly.

"I really can't believe this. How could you not know? I really think you are trying to screw with my intelligence. Is this another one of your twisted jokes? He has to look familiar to you. I know this is no coincidence Mariah! What is going on? We've been cautious, and all of a sudden a random long lost whoever shows up and you have the slightest idea who he is?"

"Oh my gosh Joey! Everything is still good to go. You're a lawyer so act like it. I mean this isn't the first dishonest incident you've taken part in. So, end the scene. The camera isn't even rolling anymore. Like sheesh, give it up! Stick your chest out, and get ahold of yourself. Acting on impulse is acting without thought and without thinking well, look where that got everyone aside from us. Baby we've been thinking and following through so what's going to stop us now? I mean okay it's a possibility that another one of my relatives has tried to sabotage me. Are you excited? Hasn't that been the case as long as you've known me? Hypothetically speaking, let's consider whichever relative that sent him is his mom or dad...okay, and? Look where that got him. They're not going to be so bold as to report him missing because we'd have them too. My journey is no secret, so why be afraid? Being dubious won't help our cause. Besides, we lived through greater scrutiny. This imbecile is clearly an amateur. I mean okay, I trusted him just like the rest but darn it how are we related and this is the furthest he got. Did he not get the full gossip on our family's olden days? Can you imagine, he's probably not even a real Journalist. Maybe he's been showing me just what he wanted me to see. Hmmm, is someone trying to challenge me? Did someone send him to give me a run for my money? Do you know what this could do for us Joey? You have to change the way you think and you'll change the way you live. This doesn't have to be negative. I just have to do slightly better with my investigating that's all. I've been under surveillance probably longer than I've been alive so that's no biggie. However, I need you to get a grip. I never asked you to compromise your career, you wanted me which means you knew there were changes that needed to be made. I'm a risk. I come with baggage… is it too much now? I'm not trying to sound ungrateful because I'm also thankful when it comes to what you've done for me. When I say I got you forever, I mean it. I won't allow anything to jeopardize your career. We're a team, let's keep it that way. But if you're going to become a chicken, let me know now and I'll be done with you. No one and nothing will get in the way of my freedom. This is nothing! Seriously it's nothing," said Mariah. "What does that even mean? How exactly do you understand the sacrifices I've made yet that easily you're ready to walk away? I helped you get away with MURDER multiple times. Do you know what that even means? Not just once, but I've helped you with each of your reporter friends because you want an attempt at fame! The audacity of you."

"If you're going to throw things in my face, at least make sure you land correctly. Joey, you didn't help me get away with murder. You helped me murder each and every one of them including the original, Aunt Elaine, so let's be real here. Let's not forget you delivered the finishing touches that ended Aunt Elaine. I took all of the fall and our plan worked, but had all of the evidence come through I doubt you'd still be where I helped to keep you until your pretend death! Your reputation, your memory...wouldn't even exist! You probably need me more than I need you right about now. Look at you, a whole lawyer shriveled up over a possible relation. Is it really that bad? Aren't you all taught how to lie? Did you forget or develop some morality all of a sudden? *Tis tis tis*. Most importantly we both know it'll go my way...or no way. You let me know what you'd like to do. Also, you're no saint. The extra hundred thousand you have just resting in your secret account isn't thanks to your debating skills in court. Your fake passing away paid you more than any company. You should be grateful. Now look at it from my view, if everything blows over and you really do die, everyone already thinks you're dead anyway.

"I thought I was making the right decision in trying to help someone that I knew potentially could be my wife," said Joey.

"Aww Joey, how sweet of you. So basically, you're saying that I've changed your mind?"

"No Mariah, I'm not saying anything. I'm telling you flat out that I think you've incriminated yourself for real this time and I'm unsure if I can sit here and watch everything we worked to keep together, fall apart. I'm saying this time I don't know if I can put your needs before my own. There's a glitch somewhere in your story and the planning is all off. How do you not know that another one of your conniving relatives is trying to set you up? I don't like messy, and this is as messy as it gets. You're asking for much more than I can afford now. Elaine got what was coming to her, but those other Journalist didn't. It hasn't even been all that long and we've created a cemetery just for your gain. This is not what I signed up for. You need help Mariah! I've done all I can for you, but enough is enough. I won't have anything held over my head. You're right I knew what I was doing too, so I'll turn myself in as well. God forgives you know. I still have other great lawyer friends and after you're given the support and attention you really need, I'm confident that I can reach out for a favor to get you the shortest time possible, said Joey."

"Do you hear yourself? I'm not doing any time, I'm sure as hell not turning myself in. Unbelievable! What a disgrace. Joey any Journalist we murdered asked for it. Think about it. They weren't trying to spread positivity about me. They were spreading lies and trying to build their blogs and following. Journalism is news. They had no news. Come on the one site said I was born in 1975 and a mother at 17. Where did that come from? We did the media a favor if you ask me," replied Mariah.

At that moment Joey storms out the bathroom and proceeds back towards the steps. When he gets to the third flight, he notices he can't see Justyce anymore. His body isn't where they left him. He starts to look all around. His heart is racing, his hands are shaking, and actual tears are forming. He yells out to Mariah, and a second later the lights go out. Joey runs toward the door, but it is locked.

"Oh Joey, I knew you couldn't hang. But, I'm not the only one," said Mariah. "Why are you doing this to me? I am your partner. Can't you see I only want what's best for you? I'm nothing like those that have hurt you. I'm trying to help you."

"Joey give me a break already. All I hear is crying and complaining. You just said you wanted to turn yourself in. This didn't just occur. You've been feeling this way. I know you Joey. You're really a good guy, you just got caught up with a bad girl. You served a great purpose in my life though. I'm sorry I wiggled my way into making you commit such hateful acts. I do appreciate you though. I always will appreciate you." "Why are you speaking as if you're not going to continue to appreciate me? What are you going to do? Don't you think it'll look funny should something happen to me Mariah?"

"Actually, I don't. Being that you had a rare heart disease and you were taking medication for some time. Remember you had a stroke, you died already. I already cried too," replied Mariah.

"What the hell are you mumbling about? I don't take any medication Mariah...you know that! And I'm not going to start," said Joey.

"Yes, you did, it's been in the cabinet. Your name is on the label. Uh oh, is someone a little late to the party? I love you forever Joey but forever is near," said Mariah.

The lights turn back on and Joey nearly faints as he sees Justyce and another familiar face coming toward him from both directions.

"I told her you were weak, I'm glad you proved me right. I guess it's about time I tell you the truth. We're not related you moron I am Justyce McCall. I told Mariah that would push you over, you helped her with murder never on your own though what a sissy. I've had a crush on her since Michael and I were little boys. Oh, you know my best friend Mike, don't you? Mike, show him the picture. He swears he knows so much about Mariah but he doesn't even know you," said Justyce. "Michael? Oh my gosh, you're working with them?" asked Joey.

"Family first, by the way it's nice to meet you. Sorry it's on these terrible terms and that we won't know each other for too long. But yes, I'm Michael Beauvoir. I am the younger cousin of Mariah, Melody, and Melissa. Justyce is my best friend. Mariah is older than we are, but we both became fascinated with her misfortune. It's funny, I didn't comprehend the burden my aunt and uncle put on her while growing up because much of the incident occurred behind closed doors. I guess because I was a child I was blinded for some time. When my parents would leave for work sometimes days at a time, I would stay at Mariah's. Justyce's family lives four houses down. They still live there today. He and I attended school together, and Mariah actually used to babysit him. But, he told me even back then that one day we'd be family for real because he was going to marry Mariah. I laughed at him because of his age and well because of you. It wasn't until recently that he showed Mariah that he deserves a chance. Mariah started noticing that you weren't fulfilling her needs and that you really need to disappear. Justyce and I have been coming over every day while you were at work for months. Once you "died" and had to spend time two towns over, we continued coming over to plan on making your disappearance authentic. While they spend time together, I've been researching different ways to successfully get her in the real spotlight. You know since you couldn't. If you haven't already guessed, Justyce knows nothing about Journalism. He lied on his resume. He went to school for business, but he didn't finish. He had an obsessive admirer some girl named Rebecca Townsend, and he used her to get his position. She saw his potential and risked her credibility to help him. Sounds like you and Rebecca could have been related huh? But once she caught onto Mariah and their chemistry, it got ugly. She put up a slight fight and covered his reputation until her final breath.

I know, it's a lot to take in. But don't worry, the others that you've offed were real for sure, however just like Justyce pretended, they actually dug too far and needed to go. Actually, look down by your feet. That's Rebecca Townsend. Wasn't she pretty? Currently that's all I'm working on, covering our steps so that curiosity doesn't kill anymore cats. So, what did

I find? The only way to assure this, is to rid the one other person that knows way too much and you're a smart man for sure. I have no doubt in my mind that you haven't already guessed that that man is you, said Michael."

"Is this a movie? No really, what is going on? You guys are both so young, and confused. Don't allow her to manipulate you. This is her art. Just look at the bigger picture. I'm her fiancé and she's willing to have you do all of this…imagine what she'll have done to you. Justyce, it's just a crush kid. You have your entire life ahead of you. Don't fall victim to her trap. She's really making you impersonate a Journalist. You all created an entire documentary and you lied about who you are. It may take time, but people will find out sooner or later. Don't let her ruin you. I had to fake my death because of her. Do you think this is something I really wanted? No, but of course I went along with it because she has me crumbled up in her chubby hand. I urge you to run! And Michael, you as well. Yes, you are family but your family means nothing to one another. If you really know your history, you should know that she has no problem getting rid of anyone. No one is exempt from her attacks. The things she said during your pretend interview may have been to expose me and my nervousness and heat, but she meant every word. If you think for a second, she won't take you guys down too you're mistaken.

Once you're no longer beneficial to her... you will go too," said Joey.

"I highly doubt it," said Justyce.

"And how can you be so certain? This is a woman I share my bed with every day and every night. I put my livelihood, my reputation, everything that I am for her on the line. I literally had to change my entire identity for her just to continue living my dream that I spent years to gain. What makes you think you're any different?" asked Joey.

"I'm aware at some point she's told you that you give her life, but she and I have created life. Believe me brother, we are different. Now please don't make this any harder than it needs to be," said Justyce.

Mariah walks into the room with her hands folded across her stomach and gazes at Justyce.

"Alright, alright, enough of the explanation. Sorry Joey, I'm really thankful but I knew you would fold under pressure even if it took a little while...I knew the day would come. You're already dead and I need all of the funds which I've already transferred into my new private account. Before you get any twisted ideas, we're really only eleven years a part. I apologize about having a child without informing you. Or should I say having a child without leaving you? Or should I be sorry for cheating. I don't know, basically I'm sorry but situations do happen. All in all, the boys are right you have to go. You know how hard I've worked, and you're unable to live up to my expectations now. I will always have love for you, but you lack edge and it has become boring. I just wanted to look you in the eyes one last time before my team sends you to your maker, and to thank you for such a great run. I swear I wish things didn't have to end this way, but above love, I was raised on survival and I feel that if we continue, I'm going to sink and I cannot have that. I hope you understand. Hell, even if you don't, it has to be done. Besides, we can't get married...that's the other thing (Mariah squeezes her finger tight smiling down at her ring yet it's different from the one given to her by Joey). Since the jig is up, I can tell you now. Justyce and I got married two weeks ago. Your ring is on the night stand, but not for long I'm going to go shopping and get my hair and nails done once I pawn it. Thank you for that as well. I figure it's the least you could do. But yes, you're now looking at *Mariah Shante Beauvoir-McCall.*

"You speak about your family, but you are your family. You are Evelyn, you are Elaine, and you are Spark. I'm not even amazed. This is what I asked for right?" asked Joey.

"Is that supposed to hurt my feelings? If so, you're going to have to come much stronger than that. Don't try to throw things that we're all more than aware of in my face. Yes, yes, the apple doesn't fall far from the tree. I'm a demon, the big bad wolf, a killer, a nightmare. Remember though you bought the dream too. Take a good look in the mirror before judging. Also remember that you're the lawyer, not the judge so it's best that you stay in your lane sweetheart. Anyway, this has gone on much longer than planned. Close your eyes so my guys can move on with your murder please and thank you."

Joey tried to say one last thing but it was too late. Justyce stabbed him five times before he fell to his knees. Michael calmly walks over and grabs some rope to tie him up. Mariah decides the stab wounds weren't enough and urges Michael to shoot an additional three bullets. She leans over to check his pulse; his body lays lifeless. The two men drag his body back to the bathroom with the hidden compartment leading to the other Journalist he and Mariah have hidden. They quickly drop him in, close the latch, and they all make their way to the living room.

"Alright boy's great work! I'll get started on dinner. Michael continue with your research we still have so much work to do. I'm feeling like a new me. Maybe it's time for a new hairstyle or a change in scenery," said Mariah.

"Now you're talking babe, let's think bigger. You have so much potential, don't allow any of this to define you, said Justyce."

"I agree cuz. Joey was holding you back. He was way too sweet. Justyce will go to war for you. As you can see, he already has," said Michael.

"Well, only time can tell. This won't be an easy ride boy, Joey was highly reputable as a lawyer. He also comes from a great family, so who knows how soon it'll be before they become suspicious should I switch up too soon. He has a lot more relatives in South Carolina. They may take the drive here. It's not my fault he couldn't keep up. I mean he served his purpose," said Mariah.

"Alright, Alright, I'm just about over talking about him. Also, my purpose better last forever," replied Justyce.

"Goodness me, don't be so silly. You all don't even compare. We are fine babe…I mean it, just fine. I told you Joey and I would be over soon enough. Did I think he'd have to die? No… I didn't think it would have to go that far but I did feel threatened. Nevertheless, with you I know I'm secured. Trust me, I have you forever," said Mariah. "Did you ever tell Joey that?"

"Excuse me!"

"It's just a simple question. Do I really hold greater value? I'm not that young, I can take it. I'm also not an idiot this answer won't change my views nor my responsibilities to you. I still know my part," said Justyce.

"I do see where you could find yourself being a bit concerned, but there's really no need. This is the only time I'm going to assure you. I guess since it is the first time you've seriously joined in and witnessed the way I prefer to move. Well Rebecca as well even though I did all of the dirty work. So, I love you babe. You're not going anywhere, just continue to be my biggest fan and we'll go far. That I can promise. Does that help at all? Ugh I feel so sappy now. You're worth it though. Just believe in me," said Mariah. "I hear you babe. You're right. Besides, I also knew what I was signing up for. It's nothing more than I can handle. You're my soft spot that's all. You're my first and last for everything," replied Justyce.

"What did you just say? I mean not like that or anything, you've never said that before. Michael's here too, I'm just shying away a bit."
"Mike knows everything. You forget the significance he holds in my life as well? Honestly, we are all thanks to him if we're being technical. And the lie about being married and pregnant was so cool. He looked like he died then," said Justyce.

"Yes dear, you're dead on. How could I ever forget? That makes you all the more special, you're family. And I know. He wasn't buying it at first. I knew that would cut deep," said Mariah. "Is that supposed to be funny cuz? He really cares for you, that's all he's trying to get at," replied Michael.

"Wow, you can't think I'm being sarcastic right now. I literally mean it from a genuine place. We are family, all of us. Both of you are being way too sensitive right now. Like really…get it together. I'm not looking to do anything to anyone especially anyone that means me well. Joey fell off and that's that! Can we move on from this already? I feel like you're both starting to worry way too much. There are more important things that we need to address. For instance, it's time to go north…New York or New Jersey. I'm sure I can keep things afloat for a few weeks but I know Joey's mother, she'll be in touch soon if she sees that I've moved on. You wanna know something ironic, he and his mother sort of have a relationship like my Daddy and Grandma Lou. Isn't that crazy, lord knows Daddy needed to detach himself from the boob. No one in their right mind would think that I would consider dating someone with even the slightest similarities but yes, I'm guilty again.

Anyway, back to what I was saying. I longed to get away from here for years but I couldn't. This is a sign, we have the chance to get up and go so let's not take it for granted," replied Mariah.

"Nothing is ever taken for granted Mariah, but when things are said or done to make me raise an eyebrow, I'm going to look for assurance. I'm not everyone else." "And no one has ever said or compared you to anyone else Justyce. Is this really the time or place?" asked Mariah.

"According to you this is the perfect time and place for everything right?" "Justyce we have company," said Mariah. "Mariah I'm not your flunkies...don't embarrass yourself." "What is your problem? Just a moment ago you said you understand what you signed up for, so what's the dilemma?" "I think you know just what you mean to me Mariah...however I don't mean the same to you," replied Justyce. "You guys let it go at least until we finish here. You both love each other. You both mean everything to one another. Now don't let your emotions slow down our purpose of all of this to begin with. Don't you think you're both becoming a bit selfish? I'm still right here you know," said Michael.

Mariah and Justyce both stood there glaring at Michael. After a while they start to smile which leads to laughter and soon turns into a makeup session. Things are back on track as Justyce runs upstairs into one of the back rooms, he lifts the twin sized bed that Mariah once called her own.

Underneath a fine layer of dust, is the small compartment the three of them used to hide their duffle bags. They packed everything needed for the perfect getaway. Mariah has multiple wigs, shoes, dresses, sweats, the guys have fancy suits, hats, fake mustaches… you name it!

CHAPTER TWO
Have You Met Karma?

Mariah, Michael, and Justyce grab their bags and head for the steps. As they begin walking down, Mariah trips and falls. Her leg slides all the way through. It's like something is tugging at it, and she can't break away. She starts to scream, and both of the guys try gaining control to help her but it is tightly caught. She has no grip, she is terrified, and feels like the walls are closing in on her. She does exactly what everyone says not to do, she starts to panic and turn red. The trepidation lasted for twelve minutes before an evil snicker slipped out. The force is released, and a young woman comes out of the darkness.

"You all seem so frightened. Did you really think there was a monster or something underneath the stairs? None of you seem that heartless. It's a joke, just a harmless prank. I need to know what I'm working with. Anyway, is Joey here? He and I have been in contact for a little while now. Did he run off? Or is he in the bathroom? Could you tell him Karma is here? I mean, if it's not too much of course... I don't mean to intrude, but he's expecting me."

"*A harmless joke*? You could have broken my leg. And we don't know anyone by the name of Karma. Why would Joey be looking for you?" asked Mariah.

If there's one thing Mariah can't stand, it's a secret. Because of her family, when involving herself with anyone under any situation or circumstance, she goes over time and time again the fact that she hates being left in the dark. But in this case, she's just being sarcastic because Karma frightened her. Karma is her sister. They recently got in touch and have been planning to meet. "Okay Mariah I get it. My joke was a bad one. Now can you please say you know who I am so that your little soldiers can lower their guards? Hi Guys I'm Karma. If Mariah mentioned me during any of your made-up interviews, it's true. I'm actually her sister on our father's side."

"Sister? I thought that part was made up. How? I'm her first cousin. I've known her, Melody, and Melissa my entire life. I've never heard your name once. Your mother isn't Evelyn. So, where did you come from all of a sudden?" asked Michael.

"My mother, her name is Avah, and our father haven't been much help. They prefer that I leave you all alone. They think it'll create more of a strain between Mariah and "Dad" should I pursue a relationship with you. My mother tried to convince me that regardless of who my father is, and despite his lack of effort that I'm hers and that's all that matters. That's the first lie I think she ever told me. But I knew even as a little girl I knew. I always felt something was off. Now I'm not trying to bash my step-father by any means. He's such a great person. He was and still is the best dad and the most honest dad that I have. He took me in as his own, and he never planned to tell me that I'm not. But that sixth sense really kicked in, I guess. I noticed at the age of seven that I didn't resemble my mother or my step-father, so I became curious. I begged her for answers but she wouldn't budge. She told me I was silly and that I looked more like my abuela Maria Alvarez. At that time, it was true I did or at least that's what the whole family agreed to. When I turned eight, things began to change... I started to look different. My features weren't like my Grandmother anymore. Not only did I start to stand out, but I started to feel different too. I felt like everyone was constantly staring at me trying to figure out who I looked like. My suspicions began to rise again, so I started hounding my mother some more. She grew frustrated, and my Dad seemed sad most of the time. It was like they wanted me to just let all of my inquiries fade and believe what they said. I tried, I really did. But then my mother had Michael and Michelle and I knew. I knew I wasn't wrong. They looked one hundred percent Peruvian. That's where I'm originally from, Peru. They didn't look mixed. They didn't look anything like me. Or I didn't look anything like them or the entire family. Yes, I had and still have the complexion, but even that's different from them. My entire look, I knew something just wasn't right. Isn't that insane? We lived so far from one another, yet we share such a similar story. That made me want to find you even more. Not only are we related, but you really relate to me. No one has ever related to me. It seems unfortunate, but it's really a blessing you know? Anyway, Michael and Michelle are twins too. They're just a bit younger than Melody and Melissa. They're literally the same except Michelle has long silky dark brown hair. Aside from that and their gender you'd think they were the same person. They were the extra push I needed in proving my case. I want to say by the time they turned five or six I asked my mother again why exactly I no longer resembled anyone. She told me I was growing into my own look, but that I still made faces and had mannerisms that mimicked her and my abuela. At that point I totally stopped buying what she was selling. My gut just felt an unbearable cramp and I knew she was holding something from me. She was just too comfortable. I felt like it didn't faze her. She treated my emotional distress like a phase and that's where the problem evolved and I couldn't let up. So, what did I do is what you're wondering right? I looked for the answer to my question and I found it! My mother and step-father planned to visit my step father's old home which was located in Cusco. He recently sold it once his mother and father passed away about four years ago. My parents made it a point to visit every few years, but this particular time I wanted them to trust me by allowing me to stay home alone. I love the city, but I was used to it and wanted to solve my mystery. We all had our own rooms, the twins were right next door to one another, my parents were across the hall, and my room was on the third floor along with my own living room space and bathroom. I checked the twin's rooms first but there was nothing there except dolls and toy cars. I checked the living room, and it was empty too. Well I did find a few quarters in between the sofa cushions but nothing major. I looked under the television stand, not a trace of anything. The kitchen cabinets only had seasonings, and the drawers had silverware. A whole bunch of fails, but I was still persistent. I wasn't sure whether or not my parents kept secrets so I figured their room wouldn't be much of any luck either. But it was still worth giving it a shot. When you assume... You make a rear end out of yourself. I was pretty close, but what I found just so saved me. Your first guess would be under the bed or in a top drawer or something right? It's okay you can say yes because that was mine. I didn't find anything just a couple of Daddy's socks and my mother's underwear. I forgot about her great fashion sense. She had dresses and blouses I hadn't seen since forever. Her shoes were always to die for. She couldn't walk too far in them but I remember she used to tell me you only need them just for a few. She said she wore them long enough to make her statement. Her wardrobe took up so much space that my father's things were almost swallowed. I grew tired looking through their clothes, so I leaned against the wall inside the closet. I remember kicking my foot back, and that's when my clue slapped me right on the back. No literally, a closed envelope fell and I jumped. Inside, was a picture of a man with my mother. He was a much darker complexion, but his face made me gasp. He looked just like me. On the back it said Beauvoir's Siempre. But wait, that's not all, a letter was attached from a woman named Spark and she knew me. She briefly explained that she was my aunt, and told me to find Mariah. She said then I'd learn who I really am. She said you beat the curse, that we were the same, and could help one another. I hid the letter, but I took the picture straight to my mother. I demanded answers. She explained to me that our father came to Peru on business. They met and instantly joined at the hip for the remainder of his trip. She said she cooked for him, she introduced him to the culture, and he told her everything that a lonely maid would believe. Of course, neither of us were there, so it's hard to tell what's honest and what's a lie, but from her tone and her words to follow, I could tell he left her emotionally scarred. She said he stayed in Peru for six days, and after that he never returned nor asked about me. She sent two letters, but he never responded. Did your mother ever mention anything? I'm not even totally sure if she knew. My mother said at the time he told her he was available, no children nor a wife. But when she didn't get a response, she said she knew better. I'm okay though. You had to have known a little about his past and trips. I doubt my mother was the first. Did you ever come across the letters when we were younger? I used my full name, it's Morgan Karma Garcia. Did you know he has other children? Are you surprised?" asked Karma.

"Oh my gosh... *Morgan Karma*, I didn't even put two and two together. Yes, I did receive them. Of course, I've been waiting for you. I just have to be sure. Sorry about that. Men lie, women lie, strangers lie, family members lie... Everyone lies. Better safe than sorry. It's my natural instinct. But it's really you! Wow, you're even prettier than I imagined. Tell me more about yourself, do you have children of your own? Are you married? How long have you been here? Do you plan to stay for a while? Have you told your mother? Of course, I remember everything now. You must excuse me there's been a lot going on today," said Mariah.

"Thank you, sister. Your thoughtful words mean so much. I've waited a long time to speak to you, to see you, and to get to know you. I know the little bit I've just shared probably seems like a lot to take in, but I'm really happy to finally be here with you. Yes, I was married for a short time to a man I knew most of my life. We lived in the same neighborhood as kids. When it was time for me to further my education, he helped in every way he could. My parents didn't have money for college, but my grades and his supportive spirit helped me significantly. This was like a win for us all. I was the first to attend college. Whenever I came home which was almost every weekend he was there. When it was time to return to school, he was still there.

We were young, not fully aware of what it meant to spend the rest of our lives with one person. He grew bored waiting for me to breakout into my career, so he filed for a divorce. I give him lots of credit because even though we didn't work out, there wasn't a scandal or any bad feeling between us. We just weren't in sync with one another's aspirations anymore. We weren't on the same page in so many important areas. He wanted quick money, an already flouring career and one child. I wanted to build everything myself so I knew it could take a little longer. I hope one day to have a really big family, but I also don't like to be rushed. All children are different and take things according to what suits their personality best, so being that we didn't work out that was a sunny side to things. Could you imagine? The generational curse would only continue. It's hard dealing with children and separating parents. No child should have to purposely go through that you know? Sometimes it's inevitable, but in other cases some parents know right away that they've seen red flags. I know I did. I didn't want to be that parent. Of course, we know it's possible and it can work, but I aspire for my children to grow in a home with both parents, totally loved, and cared for. Luckily, he still has that. He's since remarried, and has two small boys. I sent a card to congratulate them both. As for myself, I still haven't found my mister right. Actually, I'm not really doing much looking to tell you the truth. Our family has been more of my mission. Can't love someone else if I'm not head over heels in love with me, right? And how can I love me without fully knowing me right?" asked Karma.

"You're absolutely right. I'm in awe right now. It's almost like finding my own twin. I'm sorry about your discoveries, I'm sorry you were lied to. Since you're pretty much up to date with everything, you should know that if you're looking to get in touch with Daddy, I can't really help. I haven't seen him nor has my mother. We actually stopped trying to reach out. He didn't want to own up to his mistakes and that's something I couldn't really get past. Not that my mama is doing any better. She still lies too, but I will say I have at least seen her try," said Mariah.

"Oh no, he's still busy playing the victim. Believe me, I know. I had a connection that linked us together. We met, we spoke, and he literally said the same words he said to my mother. He wanted nothing to do with me. He was angry I even found him. He asked me if my mother told me what he told her all of those years ago. I said she sure did and he said well then what would bring you to come looking for me? I'd rather have no biological father than one who runs from his responsibilities. Just shows he never deserved a daughter like me anyway. Hell, I made it this far without him. What's another few decades? What's a lifetime? I'm just glad we're here together and have the chance to build a relationship between the two of us. In finding myself along this journey I've learned to appreciate what appreciates me. I don't go out my way anymore. The most work I've done and will ever do was pulling the truth from my mother. Everything else from here on out will be a breeze. I'm in search of knowing all that pertains to who I am, but I'm not forcing or going after anything that isn't for me or my growth," said Karma.

"Well ladies you're both right, this has been a mouthful. I'm so thrilled you've finally found each other, but we are actually in the middle of something... Mariah did you forget?" asked Justyce. "Let's not be so hasty. You know I didn't forget. I think we both got a little caught up that's all. It also would have been rude for me to interrupt. Plus, I didn't know half of what Karma just told us. Have some patience Hun. Where else do you have to be other than right here with me? I'm trying to let you be the man that you are, but don't test me in front of company," said Mariah.

"He's just looking out for all of our well-being Mariah. He's right, we do have an agenda to stick to. As much as I'd love to catch up on our Family tree now isn't the time. Maybe once we're settled you ladies can recap, go somewhere get a drink, or take a walk," said Michael.

"It was not my goal to disturb you fellas. Like I said, I'm here to help which means there's no need to act so jittery. I'm not a cop or a detective. I know *far more* than you think," admitted Karma.

"Oh, do you? How is that so when you've only been in touch with Joey? Do you see Joey here? Joey is dead sweetie," rebutted Justyce. "Joey knew more than you thought Justyce. In fact, I think Joey knew more than you. Or maybe is it that he was smarter than you and just knew when to stop running his mouth," spat Karma.

"I don't think you have any idea who I am. Maybe you didn't really watch the documentary so you can't tell the difference between my role on screen in comparison to what I do behind the scenes. It would be wise of you to monitor your tone. Out of respect for Mariah I'm trying my hardest not to tell you where you can go. That dramatic heartfelt story didn't move me in the least bit. To keep it groovy with you if I were Mariah, I'd ask who did you think you were to be in contact with Joey to begin with. You're not family child, we get it you want one bad but this isn't it. You're just another sick relative looking to shine through Mariah's troubles and I won't have it," said Justyce.

"Well Justyce it seems like you have me all figured out. You must have known me at least twenty years the way you're spouting out such stupidity. Mariah was right, you're a cutie but indeed you still have a lot of learning to do." Said Karma. "I thought you and Mariah were speaking through Joey. She wouldn't have described me to Joey in that way. He knew I was just the journalist and that was it," said Justyce.

"That's what I meant by you still have a lot to learn… You just don't shut up long enough. I'm not sure what my sister saw in you. No offense, but I really did watch the documentary too. I wasn't impressed. I caught your two cents sneaking out here and there. I told Mariah and I made sure she knew that if I could see through you, Joey would catch on too – sooner or later. Joey was a sad case, I thought he'd make it at least a little longer than you but needless to say you both suck equally. We can't pick sides, if Joey died what's keeping you alive?" asked Karma matter-a-factly.

"Mariah what is this woman saying? What is going on here? Michael, do you know?" asked Justyce, looking back and forth between them.

"I'm just as confused as you," replied Michael.

"Michael is telling you the truth, and so is Karma. Listen, we had a great run but you're no better than Joey. You cheated with that loser co-worker of yours which really irked me. I watched part one over too and you were a bit soft. I noticed a lack of consistency and so did Joey. He already had doubts about you. I wanted to have my cake and eat it too but now I'm full which is why I no longer needed him and I no longer need you either. Michael really is confused too, but I also know something you two think I never would. Michael, I know that you helped Justyce and Rebecca plan their first meeting which led to their first date. Please save the excuses, I don't want or need to hear anything. Let's just say everything comes back to me. Was that a secret? I believe it was. Do I tolerate secrets? I believe I don't. So, with that being said I stopped trusting either of you. Yes, Michael if you haven't caught on yet, this means you have to die too. Don't give me that look and mention nothing about family. Family doesn't help family get cheated on. I know he's your best friend, but you're my cousin! Well you were my cousin, why couldn't you be loyal?" asked Mariah.

"You just don't get tired. Who else will you have left? You're kidding?" asked Michael.

"That's what I'm wondering. This woman shows up and all of a sudden you're ready to off us both? You know what it makes perfect sense. You need help Mariah. Things are beyond what I thought. You're doing nothing but using people. If things go your way, you're happy. If someone pulls your moves on you, you're first thought is to do away with them. There are definitely some loose screws. Better yet your entire brain could use some rewiring. Are you hearing yourself? Who else is going to do the things for you that I've done? The things that we've done? Michael is your cousin for crying out loud. Michael is a cousin that you've known your entire life! He's not some fraud half-sister with a pity story trying to be you. Can't you see, she's having a whole identity crisis right before your eyes? She's not trying to help you, she's trying to be you. There is a big difference Mariah," expressed Justyce.

"You guys think you have me all figured out huh? That's totally incorrect. I don't want to be Mariah, but I do want to be here to support her. I want to show her that I have her best interest in mind unlike you two buffoons. Your idiotic mishaps have already cost her enough. Frankly it's embarrassing to continue watching the both of you carry on like this when ultimately, I'm sure you already know how things are going to end," said Karma.

"And what exactly is that supposed to mean!?" asked Michael. "Mariah don't let her do this. We've worked so hard. The three of us have worked to give you the life you crave. Don't let her do this," said Justyce.

"I'll admit, you guys have helped, but it's not enough. And it's not like you helped in a significant way or did something for her that she couldn't have done for herself. I don't know if I'd say she's been given the life she desires just yet. I think that'll be a fact once we're done here. There you go sticking your opinion in there again Mr. Writer. That's why you're not supposed to skip classes," said Karma.

"I wish things could be different. There were many instances where I tried to allow the two of you to come clean but you didn't. If you'll orchestrate something like that, I can only image what else you're capable of. I don't need snake like behavior from the two I'm supposed to confide in the most. When you lay down with dogs you get bit Justyce. And when you cross me you get ditched Michael. Don't take it personal, it's business fellas. I'm grateful for your efforts or lack thereof, but your time is up," admitted Mariah.

"You're much better than me sister I'll tell you that. When mine left me and married that bimbo I released two shots and they were both instantly gone. There was nothing to talk about. Play with my emotions, and marry the next? Who did he think he was? I don't think so buddy," said Karma.

"Wait a minute what happened to him moving on and you being understanding!?" asked Justyce.

"Oh please, did you really think I was such a calm person. I mean hello how could I be here right now if I were so understanding. And I guess I left some of the story out. As helpful as he was, while I was away studying in school, he was lending his services to my best friend Darcy. I know, isn't that just horrible, like who raised these humans? Eh such is life and that's why I took theirs. See so now it's understandable why we're going to take yours too right. Gosh, you had to make me think about it? Now I'm mad all over again," replied Karma.

"We have nothing to do with whatever you have going on. I can tell you're dejected but we're not him. Mariah knows us. It was an honest mistake," said Michael.

"Mariah doesn't know either of you. Neither of you know her either or you wouldn't have played such a risky game. That's what I'm here for. Of course, she can't get rid of you she actually cares about you two. But as for me, I could give a damn. What do you mean to me? Who are you aside from two arrogant liars that thought they could pull a fast one? *I'm here to show you why they really call me Karma.*"

Just as she did with her ex and his mistress, Karma fires two single shots killing both Michael and Justyce. Mariah's eyes begin to water but she quickly turns away before Karma can witness a single droplet. Karma smiles and jumps for joy while asking Mariah what she thinks.

"There's no going back now…" Mariah admits. She secretly wishes she could but she did feel a little better. Karma gives her a hug and tells her that it only hurts for a little while but that she's going to be much better without them around. She tells her that it's just the beginning for them and how happy she is to have found her sister. She squeezes her so tight that Mariah can barely breathe and tells her despite everything their Father didn't do, the best thing he did was give them each other. Mariah squeezes her back, thanks her for proving herself, and agrees that things will be better. The two grab their bags and place a note next to Michael that they helped him write. Apparently, he was pretty jealous of Mariah's and Justyce's relationship. He was the cousin that didn't amount to much, and wanted to be a star too. He asked Justyce about ways that he could be more hands on but Justyce ignored him. According to the letter, Michael felt that Justyce was being inconsiderate on top of being spiteful toward Mariah. He felt like he really had no future and since Justyce was unwilling to help him, he took his life right before taking his own. It would seem believable had Michael not been fired from the telephone company a few weeks back. Some cranky customer kept calling and leaving complaints her name just so happened to be Morgan. He asked about a last name to see if he could remember where she lived and when exactly he helped her, but that was all the information they had. Michael just knew helping Mariah was going to be his way out, but he didn't know literally. Mariah managed to grab ahold of her emotions while stepping over their bodies and making her way toward the door. Karma kept smiling as if she'd just won a contest. Once they both cleared the exit, Karma lit a match and tossed it. Mariah had no clue that the house she once called home would soon be nothing but ashes.

"Oh my gosh… What happened? Where did the fire come from? What did you do Karma? This isn't a part of the plan? Are you dumb? Do you want to make a spectacle of yourself!?" asked Mariah? "Whoa sister relax. Your finger prints are all over that house. Joey, Justyce, Michael and whoever else you put under are all in the house. After a while a pattern starts to develop and it's pretty easy to point out something sketchy when you're still totally fine. How is it that everyone else is disappearing except for you? Come on Mariah use your noggin! I'm just trying to help. Not for nothing but I also wanted to be a little more dramatic… you know like that movie where the wife that loses everything to her no-good husband sets his clothes on fire in the car! I can't remember the name of it for the life of me but girl that's a classic. Yeah, at that moment she was brave. I only wanted to end with a bang like that. Besides lighten up. You've done this far more times than I have. This will add an extra touch whenever you do find the right fit to interview for your real part two. I can see it now…pathetic cousin shoots journalist, lights a match, and shoots himself. If that doesn't say movie quality, I don't know what else does. Don't worry I'm humbled to have contributed there's no need to boast about me," said Karma.

"You're something else child. I tell you what I'll boast when you learn to follow direction. I appreciate your creative touch but let's stick to my command from here on out okay? You're not from here, so you don't know. It takes just one simple oops moment and we'll be doing time in a place you can't even imagine. There are so many people just waiting for me to fall short. But I didn't come this far for nothing. Like I said you're more than welcome to stick around but you have to understand that with or without help I'm the director and my production will always go on. I would like you around. But I don't need you around if you're going to do extra stuff like blowing up the house. I totally see things from you're perspective but let's not add fuel to the fire literally," said Mariah.

"My oh my do you have a way with words. I'm even more inspired. Okay you're right, back to the plan boss lady. You're in charge sister I won't let you down," said Karma.

"Great, I'm glad we're clear on things now get in the car we have a plane to catch," said Mariah.
"Now you're talking I can't wait. I'll keep it funky with you, the south is nice and all but everything is so far away. I don't know how you do it," said Karma. "What do you mean? And how are things in Peru?" asked Mariah.

"*Ha ha ha*, oh I see you're quite the comedian now. You know only my Grandmother lived there. I've never even had the opportunity to see for myself. New York is very busy though. I'm

used to being up and out constantly. Maybe one day once were living the way we really should we can really take a trip to Peru," said Karma.
"It took everything in me not to cry hysterically when you were telling that story. I don't know why you had to be so riveting. But yes, Karma that sounds like fun to me. Hopefully we live to see the day, we can actually take a trip there," said Mariah.

"In my former life I was an actress so what do you expect? I just wanted to spice things up a bit. It's not like I lied, my mother's side is really from there." "Yeah but you're from New York," laughed Mariah.

"Okay. and you shop at stores called the Piggly Wiggly. Am I laughing?" asked Karma.

"No, you're not laughing, you actually look like you're about to sob. Simmer down child it's just a joke. You're roots trace there and one day you will get the opportunity to see it. I wasn't trying to torment you. Also New York is where dreams come true so be proud," said Mariah.

"I guess all except mine. How come my dreams never came true then? This the closest I ever got to acting and its real life. So, can you explain that...?" inquired Karma. "We both know you had a few bad breaks but you can't keep holding onto the past or you'll live there forever.

Sometimes our plans aren't always God's plans," said Mariah. "How inspiring, did you discover that before or after I lit the match," mocked Karma. "You sure do like testing my patience child. I was only trying to lift you up since you magically forgot where you're really from. But since your smart tongue shows you're feeling better, let's continue," replied Mariah.

"I didn't mean anything by it. My guard is always up but it's not your fault. We have a job to keep to. That's why I'm here, and that's what I must keep reminding myself. So, don't mind me boss lady. I'm ready to go now," said Karma.

"Well let's go then… Safety first buckle up," said Mariah. "You got it sister, I'm all set," replied Karma.

Karma styles her hair into three French braids, kicks off her suede brown boots and reclines her seat. Mariah twists her hair and digs for her bag on the floor next to Karma. She pulls out a pair of brown shades, a brunette bob wig, and a royal blue dress shirt. She kicks off her sneakers and switches into a pair of boots. Both women look at each other, toss their heads back, and start cackling at each other's thirty second transformations.

"Did we really do it? You think we're really going to get away with it?" asked Karma.

"We did, and we absolutely have already gotten away with it. Don't ever underestimate me," insisted Mariah. "I wasn't underestimating you. I was simply asking a question. This is still all so new for me," said Karma.

"How so? Again, we've already established what happened to your husband," said Mariah.

"Yes, but that was different. Also, I never finished explaining to you. I have to come clean. I was there for the shooting and I held the gun right after the incident but I did have some assistance," said Karma.

"Help how? Help from who? Are you lying again? Don't start your mess Karma."

"This is the honest truth. I was seeing someone too. I could feel things were changing so I made a friend of my own. His name was Kyle Lankston. We attended college together. I thought he was crazy about me but come to find out he was just crazy. I told him about what was going on and it was actually all his idea. He said they were sinners and the world would be better without them. I thought well look at that ask and you shall receive. I didn't even have to do much," said Karma.

"Interesting… So, that means you're really a punk? You've really never done anything like this before? How did you get the nerve with Michael and Justyce then? And what happened with Kyle? Where is he now? I really can't believe you. You're just full of lies huh child," mocked Mariah.

"That's why I was so into making a scene at the house. It was basically a world premier for me. I'm not that kind of person, but you showed me that I could be if I needed to. I got the nerve because I wanted to impress you. As far as Kyle, he caught a bad case of Karma. I swear I'm not trying to be funny. A month later he was in the paper. A psychotic husband did him in after finding out he had an affair with his wife. I was totally appalled. If he wasn't the pot calling the kettle black. I remember thinking some nerve. But to answer your question he's somewhere six feet under. I didn't know much about his personal life or family so I chose not to reach out. Secretly I just thanked him for doing me a solid favor and prayed for his loved ones. I guess my karma was the fact that he was having relations with me and that married woman at the same time. So, while he was consoling me for what my husband did, he did as well. I just never found out while he was still alive. What a good old dirty dog I tell ya," said Karma.

"Sheesh girl! I think you're right! We really are related. I'm sorry you had to go through all that. One thing my mama used to tell me is God don't like ugly. So sometimes people get what's coming to them. Guess Kyle forgot about his own sins and didn't know the world didn't need that kind of energy either. No man is worth that kind of stress. So, that other husband that took matters into his own hands I'd say helped you the most. I'm glad you decided to open up. I don't think you're a punk anymore. But from here on out if we're going to be hanging and doing these shenanigans together... I need you to be totally honest with me. I don't do riddles and mysteries. I prefer you be blunt and up front with me. Keeping things away from me is the easiest way for me to keep my distance from you. I respect you and the things you've gone through. I'd like that same respect in return and that means always telling me the absolute truth. I don't care how unappealing it may be if it's the truth I will always respect it. A lie is created when someone is trying to cover something up. Think about it...look at everything you already know about me. There is no need for you to ever feel like you can't be yourself, open up, or at the very minimum tell me the truth. That's what I'd do if the shoe were on the other foot. Outside of being your sister, I'm a person. Every person deserves the truth. You and I both know this. DO I HAVE YOUR WORD?! I mean it, don't just say it because you think it's what I'd like to hear. If not, we can stop right here, I'll drop you off somewhere and from there you can carry on. I'm never the type to throw a person under the bus so you'd be fine should you choose to move on without me," said Mariah.

"You have my word Mariah. Just as you have to feel people out so do I. I mean right away I knew we connected without even being raised together. But I still wasn't sure how you were going to receive me. I wasn't sure if you were even going to receive me period. I see now that what happened at the house was a test. I hope I showed you that I can pass with flying colors. Yes, I'm not as experienced in this area as you thought but that should be all the more reason that you can really confide in me. I will always pass whatever task is at hand without a doubt. I mean it Mariah, you can count on me. I won't let you down.

"Alright, I've warned you. I've given you a fair chance so we shall see. I hope that you don't make me regret it because from here on out there's no turning back. The only outcome after this moment should you choose to betray me will be the same as the others. As you saw Michael was my cousin, much more like my brother. We actually did grow up together and well look what happened. I have a way with getting exactly what I want. I can also see weakness before it hits me. Please, don't try me for your sake more than mine," said Mariah.

"You have my word," replied Karma.

CHAPTER THREE
Everyone Likes Road Trips

Mariah stares at Karma for a few minutes to see if her facial expression will change, indicating a possible lie. Karma places her hand on top of hers instead and reassures her, explaining that she has nothing to worry about. She says she really understands, she's an actual team player, and that real family won't let you down. Then, she turns the radio to KYSS FM and starts to jam out. Mariah says okay and for the millionth time puts a heavy emphasis on the warning to her. Then she turns the radio up and joins in on the song. Mariah has listened to KYSS FM since she was a little girl riding up and down the country roads with her mama. While her father was at work and before the twins came along, she and her mama would drive for hours running errands and sometimes just to get some air and hear the tunes played on the radio. In between commercials Mariah expresses to Karma the importance of the radio. She tells her that music is the one thing that kept everyone in her household going. She tells her that their daddy was big on funk. He could be in the middle of a heated argument. Someone could be confronting him about the craziest of subjects, and you throw on one of his songs and he'd be ready to dance. She told her he'd probably have that enemy ready to dance right along with him. That's the thing, although he wasn't the greatest to his family, most people on the outside looking in really admired him. Growing up he'd do lots of nice things for other people. Like that one time on Smith Street when an older couple broke down just before the light. He hopped right out of his truck and helped the man push his car to the gas station. He used to help women with their groceries to the car, donated to all the girl scouts, didn't like church much, but still sent in his tithes and offerings as faithfully as the next member.

That reminded Mariah of another story. She turns the radio down some and starts to cheese reminiscing about this particular story. Every Sunday she said her mama would get them all dressed for church. She on the other hand attended regularly. Mariah said her mama knew that their daddy would refuse, but she still asked each week if he wanted to go too. Although he made it such a battle, Preacher Perry told her mama that some people come to God a little later, but her job as his wife was to never give up. Mariah told Karma that she didn't agree with that. She told her that in her mind she always thought their daddy should have already been faithful to God and maybe he would have been faithful to their mama. But as quickly as she said it, she took it back because she thought…

Well, then what was her mama's excuse?

Mariah starts giggling thinking about the next part. Karma gives a weird hoot in return and scratches the side of her head as she waits for her to continue. Mariah says that one day their daddy decided to surprise them at church. He wanted to see what all the hype was about. When he got there, service was just beginning. He sat in the back on the left-hand side which was the same side as the preacher. There was a total of 18 rows on both sides, a purple carpet, and scriptures all throughout the aisles. The ushers were on each side of the building, and almost everyone in the room greeted him just as soon as he came in. Everyone except Mr. Marshall. Mr. Marshall was this fine golden bronze man with shiny red hair. He wasn't married, and he never skipped a Sunday just like Evelyn. She said their daddy spotted him all womanless and made sure he stayed until the end of service. Her mama never did notice. As the congregation made their way back out the glass doors, Mariah said everyone waved except Mr. Marshall. He came over and gave her mama a nice big hug. Her Daddy saw that, and he didn't skip but one or two more

Sundays from there on out. Mariah slapped her thigh she was so tickled.

"My mama used to sing to us all the time. I remember her soulful voice like it was yesterday. She liked a few songs of the world, but mostly the ones she learned in the choir. Boy, did she really love going to church. It's almost unbelievable she was so faithful to the organization but not to daddy, well not to me. It's like God is up here, and slightly below was right where I placed her. The world could say mama did this or that and I'd say, *you liar not my mama*. I would ride for her until the wheels fell off. She's so different now though. Don't even look or sound the same. Face still pretty though, but her spirit took a bruising for sure… so, did mine," admitted Mariah.

"I'm so sorry about your mama. I didn't mean to shift your mood with this music. Once upon a time I used to sing too. I have an aunt on my step-father's side named Taylor Lattimoore," "Oh my gosh I'm familiar with her music," said Mariah.

"Yes, her maiden name is Garcia. But she's been singing since before my time. She said she would take me under her wing if I was serious. I told her about as serious as a stroke. Child, I would have been foolish to let an opportunity like that pass me by, right? At least that's what I thought. As an 18-year-old girl at the time I admit I was a bit naïve. With my lack of confidence, you could have told me anything. Which is what she did. She said if I gave her $100 every other week, she'd use that money to get me bookings. Now what teen girl wouldn't jump out of her socks? Before she could hardly finish speaking, I already saw bright lights and my name lit up all over New York City. But it didn't last like I thought it would. I found out down the line that she got lots of venues, but for her daughter," said Karma.

"Are you kidding me child? Wow, I know you gave her a piece of your mind with due time, didn't you?" asked Mariah.

"I wish I did now, but then I only wanted peace in my mind so I told her to keep it. I figured she needed it more than I did to do something so underhanded. Plus, her daughter couldn't hold a tune. Voice could break three mirrors at once. People got over her pretty face in about three seconds of her singing," said Karma.

"That was a good one, I needed that," replied Mariah. "I'm glad I could help. That's all I ever want to do is help. I know it's hard to take in, I know you're scared or if you'd prefer cautious, but I'm really genuine. When I found out about you Melody and Melissa, I was thankful. I don't want anything from you or even from the girls other than to build a friendship and hopefully with time sisterhood. The same way you've been stabbed in the back, so have I. But regardless of those that have tried to come against you, you can't block out those that are meant for you," said Karma.

"That means a lot Karma. I'm trying, believe me if you really know me, you'd know you and I are making great progress. I don't accept easily but having you here in my space isn't so bad after all. However, this is still just the beginning. You haven't been presented with any serious test yet. With or without you Michael and Justyce both had it coming. I can shout teamwork with you, but I'm still a force by myself. There is no such thing as pulling a fast one over on me and getting away with it. I don't care how long it takes me. I will find out and when I do, I'll act on my instinct accordingly. This is not to come off in an arrogant way. Like I said I didn't always view things as I do now. Just continuing to make lemonade with my lemons," said Mariah.

"True indeed, but remember to grow through what you go through. Those terrifying events led you to where you are now. You needed them. Mentally you already beat the **curse.** Don't let it secretly hold your emotions hostage. I'm rooting for you, but you have to root for you just a little bit louder," said Karma.

"I hear you child… Thank you," said Mariah.

"Anytime don't mention it," said Karma.

North Carolina is bigger than they think. They've been talking so much that it didn't even register that they are barely getting anywhere. Seems like the town is never ending. The plan was to drive straight to the airport, but on the radio, they said that the cops were circling the perimeter looking for a suspect for a gas station crime in Raleigh. The girls' figure there's no need to fall behind nor get caught in a trap so it's in their best interest to stay far away from the police as possible.

Besides, *everyone enjoys a road trip, right?*

The sun is starting to sneak out, the wind is running wild. Mariah and Karma debate over where to go and finally agreed on Pennsylvania. New Jersey was Mariah's choice but Karma isn't so interested. New York was Karma's choice but Mariah decides to pass. So, looks like Philly is the happy medium. Neither of them has ever been to Pennsylvania before but Mariah remembers hearing their Daddy talk about visiting distant cousins. She never got to go with him, so she put it on her bucket list. The 76ers are from Philly. They're one of Mariah's Favorite basketball teams. Seeing them play is another bullet on her bucket list. "I'm delighted we chose Philly. Think about it I can get an actual Philly cheesesteak from Philly. Of course, we have them in New York but who doesn't want to go the namesake. Aren't you ecstatic?" asked Karma. "It's rather intriguing the things that bring you happiness. I swear you don't get out enough. I mean I've never been to Philadelphia either but a cheesesteak... really? Don't we have better things to focus on right about now? More important things? You can get a cheesesteak from the Piggly Wiggly girl?" said Mariah.

"Girl there is nothing more important than a good meal. I'm all for work too but let's be realistic here. Plus, we just got here. Can we enjoy the moment before you go being so serious?" asked Karma. "Sure, we can but you're going to enjoy every moment with a lifelong cell mate if you don't start using your head and remembering the bigger picture. My house, the only one I've ever called home is now crispier than a potato chip thanks to your wonderful artistic skills. But what matters more is what was in the house and who discovered the house. Unlike you, I've been alert and paying attention to what's happening around us. I've been listening to the news. Reporters and officials are all over Raleigh right now looking for a suspect which almost fits your description," said Mariah.

"My description? What do you mean? How? Who saw us!? When?" asked Karma.

"Oh, I see you're full of questions now. I mean, when you lit that match and decided to have your premature exhale moment, you weren't alone. Someone was watching and they saw enough to describe you more than they should be able to. There's no us, they saw you," said Mariah.

"I'm lost, is that some sort of subliminal? This is not my fault. I did what you asked. I got rid of the problem. Whoever thinks they saw me didn't see a thing. This can be fixed. We're a team. It just happened, you said the police department is incompetent. So, what do they really know?" asked Karma.

"I'm being direct with you. A subliminal means I'm nervous about saying what's exactly on my mind. That's never been my case. I try to educate you, I try to let you in just a pinch but deep down I know you're a screw up. Look at this, just another mess," said Mariah. "You know something, everyone is right about you. You're just a sad piece of work. You really do use people up and toss them in the trash just as soon as you get the opportunity. What are you some sort of lead singer? Do you think you're a solo artist? Who died and made you perfect? It works as long as we can live out your sick fantasies, right? If Mariah is joyful, Mariah is fine. You call everyone belittling names, but you're the weakest one of us all. *Do you know that*? You don't care, you don't have feelings, and nothing anyone ever does will ever be enough! Why!? I know exactly why, it's because of your own insecurities. You weren't enough for your mother. She didn't care about you enough to leave Dad. That's where all this animosity comes from. You weren't enough for him either. You can't keep blaming the world. How about you start being accountable and get the hell over it already. You're a grown woman now. Hell, you should be someone's mother already but no because if you do that, they might be more important than your fixation on being this deprived and pathetic girl. Oh, me oh my… *why oh why*. Give me a freaking break already!" spat Karma.

"Nicely ask someone how they feel and they'll say fine. Get someone mad and you'll get the truth," said Mariah. "And here you go with another equation. I graduated long ago. What are you rattling about now?" asked Karma.

Mariah pauses and turns her head away from Karma. She can see that Karma is annoyed because she isn't responding to her right away. Her eyes are closed and she's counting backwards from twenty. She's moving her shoulders up and down and sliding her birthstone colored ring back and forth on her ring finger of her right hand. Happy thoughts, happy thoughts she keeps repeating. She's uses this practice in therapy almost every other visit. Dr. Pressleigh says it's a considerate way to tap out of a conversation without being confrontational. You don't warn the person, you don't argue, you just start counting. At some point they should understand. Not Karma...she's yelling at the top of her lungs. She keeps calling Mariah inconsiderate, crazy, manipulative, deranged, and strange. Mariah keeps counting. Karma turns the music up louder and tries to drown her out. Mariah Is still determined to clear her thoughts. Karma's really mad now. She tugs at Mariah's hair and demands her to converse with her like a civilized adult. Mariah burns her soul with her eyes. "You weren't on the radio you nincompoop. Time is precious, I'm not about to let you waste mine. There's a difference between wanting to be like someone and wanting to be them. If all you said is how you actually feel about me then I can't help but to question your reason for sticking around. Now I know that little drop of a mind of yours is sure confused right now. But this was your test which I told you was coming, and child you **failed** terribly. Do you know who I am? Do you know who you're talking to? Are you aware of what you've gotten yourself into? You've mentioned a lot of considerable theories. It's true I'm still not so over the past. What can I say? Some things just don't go away. But I don't know who you think you're talking to like that. If they were talking about you on the radio I would fear for my life. You're despicable. You'll never make it in this army. And disturb my prayer session again and I'll pray after I find a place to hide your body," said Mariah.

"This was a test? There really is something wrong with you. Like I said I don't know what your motive is or where you see yourself or even your life, but you need some serious help girl. The way your mind twists and turns you're bound to head right off the road. I said a lot. Some I meant. Some I didn't… it was out of anger. Can you see how you contributed? You and I both know how annoying it is to be doubted. Do you ever own up to anything!? I didn't give you any reason to trick me like that. It was uncalled for. But I'm still totally in Mariah. Sometimes people have disagreements and that's normal. It doesn't mean you always have to terminate the person. I got angry you would have too. You made me feel ignorant. You made me feel just like everyone else when all I'm trying to do is prove to you that I can keep up and get things done without being a hindrance. Be reasonable, we both over reacted and provoked one another. Let's both take blame for our actions and move on in the right direction. Remember we have a whole journey ahead," said Karma.

"That all sounds really good. It would have sounded better had you not tried to embellish on my trauma. I don't need a life coach sugar and if

I did, she wouldn't be you. Thank you, but it's not called for," said Mariah.

"I'm trying…"

"Trying what girl? That's what you don't get. I don't need anyone in my camp that tries. I'm a doer. Either you do or you don't, and you don't do anything for me with your sorry excuses! Pick your head up, have some pride. See what I mean! Weak! I can't afford a risk like you," admitted Mariah.

"Out of respect… I'm *really* trying."

"There you go again," said Mariah "Alright then I won't try. You've got it all planned out, so what happens now boss?" asked Karma.

"Well I thought you'd never ask. So, in a couple of days things are going to actually heat up. Currently News 12 has very few details but they do know for sure that there was foul play in the fire. This news update is real not like the one I just made up that terrified you. You were trying to drown my prayer and missed the reporter over the radio. He said the house didn't burn to a crisp thanks to Joey's sturdy techniques in case of an emergency meaning they've discovered some evidence. They can't trace anything just yet however a few of the bodies in the basement belong to the media. I needed the right Journalist but they just kept crossing me. But how could I let them go knowing the things they knew. They would have ruined me! Anyway, that's what we are dealing with right now," said Mariah.

"So, we're a WE again? What does any of this information have to do with me? Where do I come into play? What are you expecting me to do or say?" asked Karma.

"The scenario that I caused you to lash out over could have easily been true. Most likely the media will try to make matters much worse than they are. If they find a suspect for whatever reason if they believe you have something to do with the incident, you won't face as harsh consequences as I would. I've already dealt with the court system, now Joey, Justyce, and Michael are all dead…it won't look good," said Mariah.

"Lots of things don't always look good. I'm still not sure what you're saying. Can you clarify?" asked Karma. "I did the bulk of the work. It was all premeditated, but I didn't force you to join in. It was your own impulse that pushed you. You wanted to feel what it was like. You wanted to indulge in the curse just as much as the rest of the family," said Mariah.

"Hold on just one second here, are you trying to make me take the fall?" asked Karma.

"I'm trying to make you take a leap."

"A leap into where, a burning hot pit? Do you hear yourself Mariah? Listen I don't know what all you think you heard on that radio of yours but I'm telling you now I will not take the blame especially by myself," said Karma.

"I wasn't asking you... I'm telling you dear. Think about the options you have go down willingly or vanish," said Mariah. "Who said I am going to run? I don't plan on going anywhere," said Karma.

"Oh, but you will. That's what the letter says the one you left by my suitcase," said Mariah. "You're a whole Nutcase, I didn't write any letter! What kind of a fast one are you trying to pull here!? You're really beginning to disturb me. Are you hearing yourself? Look I'm not doing or agreeing to anything so I guess you'll just have to do to me as you did to the others when the time calls for it," said Karma.

"I really hope you don't think that is some sort of reverse strategy. Sweetie dear sweetie I don't need your approval. I know my power, my strengths, my abilities...when I'm ready so will you," said Mariah. "Outrageous is what you are! Throw you and the entire mind away. I'm serious, I don't know what your mama was on when she had you but child I'm bewildered.

You're a two-way trip all by yourself. I can't believe I allowed myself to fall into your trap, your web of lies. All you're doing is allowing the one or two same encounters you've gone through fuel a killing spree which you don't even carry out yourself. You know what you're doing though. You make everyone that crosses paths with you out to be your follower and you feed off of their sympathy. Well, Mariah... I'm all sympathized out. You get what you get and you don't get upset," said Karma.

"I remember now who you sound like. If I didn't know I'd think you were related to Elaine too. She was the one person that could grind my nerve without even trying. It's a shame she's not here to tell her side of the story... be careful child," said Mariah. "So, she slept with our dad oh gosh big whoop! Here you go again back down memory lane. This whole story of yours is getting tired. Just have your way already I'm sick of the anticipation. Whatever you're going to do you're going to do anyway. I won't gravel...not now, not ever. It's not necessary, nothing you've done has been necessary. I only wish I never came to Raleigh. You country folks are weird. We don't play this in New York. Bet I take you back home you'd act right fairly quick," said Karma.

"Is this the part where I'm supposed to wail? It's so funny once I'm ready to send you all to your maker, everyone grows this courage in trying to tear me down. I'll tell you just like I told them, save it. Your thoughts don't pay my bills. I didn't request for you to come looking for me. You sought out Joey if I recall correctly," said Mariah. "But what really changed? There's something else you're holding back isn't there? If the police are already making statements, it's only a matter of time before they make their way to you with or without me. You're connected to everyone that was burned in the house. Why would you want to add onto your already tainted image?" asked Karma. "Your lack of intelligence is showing again. I've come this far. I know what I'm doing. The question is how much further do you think you're going to make it? Pick me pick me, I know the answer," said Mariah.

"We haven't even seen Philadelphia yet. Who needs this hostility? Maybe you just need to get out, smell some fresh air, have a bite to eat, and think about things other than your personal life," said Karma. "All of your concerns and suggestions have been helpful seriously… NOT. You're killing me, just kidding I'm killing you. I made a funny. But this is it, close your eyes I'll make it quick." As Karma closes her eyes Mariah leans toward her with a plastic bag. She grabs her hair neatly and places into a ponytail. Right before she puts the bag over Karma's head, Karma ducks. At this point she's trying to break free from the car which is pulled over on the side of the road but the door is jammed and won't let her free. Mariah tells her to hold still, that she won't feel a thing. Karma knows better. They tussle for about five minutes and finally Karma is defeated. Mariah knocks her out, strangles her, and turns the radio back up. If anything, she's disappointed. She thought Karma was soft, but not that bad. She drives with her body reclined back until making it to the next rest stop. Then, she slides Karma in the trunk through her back seats. Pennsylvania is still a long way from where she is right now.

CHAPTER FOUR
The Show Will Always Go On

Dear Diary,

I think I made a mistake marrying my husband. I don't think he's the person that I thought he was. I don't think I'm the woman he really needs either. I stood before God and I swore that I would be a devoted wife but I haven't felt loved since that very day. I chose not to tell my husband about these feelings instead I stepped out on our marriage. But I know he's not happy either. I'm not blind, I'm not deaf, and my sense of smell is awakened every time my nose grazes her cheap scent on the collar of his shirts. I've thought about bringing it up just to see what he'd say. Would he have an excuse? Would he tell me the truth? I always change my mind because I'm just as guilty. Wouldn't that make me a hypocrite? What about you God? Would that change our relationship? Will you love me less? My other reason, my children. I stay for them. I don't want them to think I've given up on our family. I don't want them to know a home without both parents. But I know deep down that they can feel in a way that I've disconnected from their father. Mariah sees things. She's says things that implies that she's wiser beyond her years. She's told me to put my happiness before theirs but, how can I? I am the mother, they come first and that's it. I thought about it once. I was packed and ready to go. Then Mariah's teacher called and said she was misbehaving in class. She asked me if anything changed at home. My husband was sleeping on the couch, we were barely speaking and our relationship became a symbol of survival. Well a more obvious symbol. We ain't stood for love in a long time. Knowing it affected Mariah I had no choice but to work on my acting... the marriage changed me. I stopped living thinking this will help my child. Unintentionally I've been destroying the both of us. There's no growth in a comfort zone especially a fake one. I hope one day that Mariah will see I really did give my all and I'm sorry that her father and I fell short. I pray none of our wrong doings impacts her future decisions in a negative way.

-Evelyn Beauvoir

The drive wasn't so bad by herself but it would have been really helpful if Karma didn't flake and ruin everything. Mariah is feeling the pressure, but it doesn't stop her from making it to her destination. She passes two signs that welcome her to Pennsylvania, two gas stations, some stores, and the one thing she needed the most, a motel. Mariah sits on the bed with her legs stretched out slightly above Karma's hips. Karma is placed horizontally at the end. Mariah's petite stature gives more than enough room for the both of them to fit comfortably. Looking at Karma is making her upset all over again. She decides to take a moment to pray again. She is able to eliminate all distractions except the deep voice on the TV that yanks her attention. It belongs to James Dexter, a local News Reporter from Raleigh. He decides to interrupt the regularly scheduled game show with an update from back home...

"This just in, we've got more details on the fire that occurred at the infamous Beauvoir home located on Ashe Ave here in Raleigh North Carolina. As of right now officials have no clear motive. But I had the chance to speak with the Prezscott's two houses over and the Sanderson's across the street. Both Couples say the fire comes as a surprise, that it must have been an accident, and lots of other great things about the family. As of right now details are still developing. We'll be sure to keep you updated as the story progresses... Back to you, Lury..."

Mariah got so upset she kicked Karma off the end of the bed resulting in a big thump. Her leg twisted, if she were still alive it probably wouldn't have been a good sign. Mariah jumps down stepping right over her and begins putting her things back in her bag. She opens up Karma's too to see if there is anything of use. She only has a few more wigs, pants, and an unlabeled envelope. Of course, Mariah is eager to see what is inside so she opens it up. There she finds a receipt for $20,000 and a stack of hundred-dollar bills. She couldn't take it all in to solve where the money came from and what she was planning to do with it so she closes it back up and puts it into her duffel. She takes the extra pants and wigs as well. She thinks that she could never have too many personalities especially in her field of work. She is almost on her way back out when she spots a blue pair of scissors on the wooden nightstand. She picks them up and stands in front of a body length old fashioned mirror in the room. She starts pulling in her hair styling it in a different way and then out of nowhere she randomly snips a chunk from the left side. To even it out she has to do the right. Then she goes for the back and then the bangs which use to cover her forehead and her eyebrows, no longer exist. The trim quickly becomes a full-blown buzz cut. She keeps going until she can't go any further. Then she grabs an old baseball cap of Joey's. It was his good luck charm one of his Professor's gave him in law school. She starts to smile remembering the pride he had every time he wore it. For the brief moment she missed his voice, his touch, overall his entire presence. As she pulls the strap to make the hat tighter, she slaps her cheeks to snap herself out of the mushy moment and snatches back control of her wondering mind. Then she pulls out a jacket, another pair of tall boots, and a natural colored lip gloss and heads for the exit. She didn't think Karma needed to come along for the next ride. She wasn't ready and well Mariah had a schedule to stick to so she figured the show must go on…

Maybe next life, perhaps?

She left the body there underneath the bed with a letter explaining why Karma "gave up". She doesn't see the need in returning the room keys. She thinks going back to the hotel lobby and conversing with anyone could create a bigger catastrophe if they are able to identify her later on down the line. So, she left the keys right next to Karma should she decide to change her mind and come on back to life. As she walks over to the car with the key in her hand she hesitates for a few seconds. She and Karma arrived in that car together and although she almost looks like a totally different person with her current edgy tom boy appearance, there's always one nosy neighbor a little more aware of what's going on than others. Mariah steps back from the car and starts walking off of the premises. She zips up her coat and makes her way toward the light. Looking up at the buildings she sees the first street sign which reads Crestmont Avenue. It's not like any of them would ring a bell being that she's so far from home, but she decides to go ahead and give it a shot. Looks like there are a couple of different stores she can check out. The first one she stops by is called 'WE GOT YOU: Food & Treats.'

"I don't know why I chose to listen to her. I don't know anything about Pennsylvania. I've read about New Jersey plenty of times. She didn't even make it a whole week. I should have just trusted my gut. But no no look at me now, more chaos because of another family member. Does it ever end? I wish the twins were here with me. They'd at least know how to cheer me up. They're both still kicking butt in the corporate world. I wonder if either of them have heard from Mama or daddy. They really don't need to. We're all better off not speaking because it never goes well. There's still too much damage to get past the hello. I'm doing it again. I can feel it. I just wish somehow some way but I know it's not possible. It's going to take a while for me to remove Karma's face. I'm still working on Elaine that evil woman pops up every so often. She belittled me, mama, my daddy, and anyone else she could get her hands on. I felt bad at first but Joey and I did the world a favor I swear. I kind of miss Joey just a little. He didn't care what I did, he really

loved me. Or maybe it's because he lacked in the same areas and couldn't love himself too. He would have denied it, but I know he knew about Justyce and myself. He probably knew about my other dinners every so often too. He just wouldn't confront me. I don't think he wanted to acknowledge me in that way or to say that everyone was right about me. Justyce was pretty great too. He really was an amazing actor and overall persuasive person. He had one of the top positions at the news station without a degree. Rebecca really liked him too huh? He just couldn't get with my program. I'm not sure who or what gave him the impression that he could cheat on me and everything would still be peachy cream. That's where he messed up. Michael was the one relative I knew was in my corner. I thought he had my back but he was only pushing the knife a little deeper. This is why they all had to go. I'm not wrong. I know I'm not. You can't tear someone down and expect no result in return. And how else would it have ended? I could have left the relationships, right? But then how do I really win? How do they feel my pain? How do they comprehend the seriousness of their actions without some sort of backlash? If you think about it just as I warned Karma, I've warned everyone just don't cross me and no one gets hurt. Did any of them take heed? Or did they take my kindness for weakness? I read something once where it said you only have to tell someone something once. Should you tell them again, it means they didn't respect you nor your wishes from the beginning. I felt that then, and I feel that now. There is nothing more heartbreaking than having your heart broken again by someone that knows about the first heart break to begin with. Think about it, they all knew what was troubling me. So why provoke me to go back to a place or a person that I no longer want to be? I'll tell you why because it's a board game. People find humor in watching other people fall. They like drama, they don't really care about what you're going through. They just want to know. Everyone loves a juicy tale at the expense of others. I didn't harm mama or daddy the two where everything originates from but think about Elaine's motive to hurt mama. It wasn't her house that was turned upside down. It all makes sense just think about it. I tell you what though. I refuse to go to anyone's jail no sir not Mariah. I know my rights. I've done lots of great deeds. I have to snap out of it and follow through with my original plan before Karma creeps in the way. I can still do this. I can still make it happen. It's not over. I'm still just getting started. I'm still fighting back. I'm still cursing the curse that tried to curse me. I'm still ahead. I can make it through Pennsylvania and wherever else my expedition leads to. I won't get captured and no one will stop me. I'm Mariah Shante Beauvoir...

I'm not my past. I got this."

"I'm sorry ma'am did you say something?" asked the cashier, confused.

"Oh! Heavens no! I apologize sugar I was just speaking out loud to myself. A little positive self-talk that's all. How much did you say everything will be again?" asked Mariah. "No problem at all ma'am. It's $12.12 please," replied the Cashier.

"Well isn't that a lucky number. I may have to play the lottery tonight. Don't you think? Drew is it? Is that short for Andrew? Goodness I didn't notice there is a crowd forming behind me. I don't mean to hold up your line. Keep the change sweetie and thank you for your help," said Mariah. "You're fine ma'am, it's not an issue. I'm sure everyone is okay with waiting their turn. You look very familiar but I've never seen you around here before. I don't believe you gave me your name either," said Andrew. "Well how rude of me. I'm from North Carolina and my name is Mariah. Is that better?" asked Mariah. "That's actually much better. I'd like to get to know you a little better. Maybe we could share a second conversation over dinner. I'll cook!" Mariah smiled. "And I'll eat, you've got yourself a date sugar," said Mariah. "Awesome we could meet back here around 7. I guess that'll give you time to take care of whatever errands you may have and stop home to freshen up a tad," replied Andrew. "Yes, that's a splendid idea. Take care of business and stop home. Hmm home…"

"Is there something wrong with home," asked Andrew?

"Oh of course not. I'm sorry just thinking to myself again. But yes, seven is perfect I'll see you then," said Mariah.

Mariah left out of the store contemplating on a location where she could change her clothes and relax for the next few hours. Almost every store looks obvious. Coming in with a rugged demeanor and leaving out totally different would probably stir the pot again. Her body starts to shut down from all of the walking when she spots another small motel off to the back of a street by itself. She walks in and rings the old-fashioned bell for assistance but of course it doesn't work. She begins to look around and she sees actual holes in the walls. People would always refer to a not so nice place as a hole in the wall, but these are real holes. The green carpet looks like it could use some attention, and the wooden chairs and table coupled with whatever animal the owner probably ate half of hanging on the wall gives off a real-life thriller movie feel. On the counter there's a sign in sheet and a note in big bold print that reads 'NO REFUNDS.' Hanging almost above her head is a broken ticking clock, and all the way to the left underneath three holes, are sets of different keys. Mariah steps back and takes a deep breath unsure of what she walked into. "Is this real? Why does everything look so vintage," she thought to herself. After approximately three minutes, a small older woman with dark red hair, a black dress, a light weighted sweater and black flat shoes comes to the front desk. Before she says hello, she yells out "I know you from somewhere!" She's so excited as if Mariah were a celebrity, that she can barely compose herself.

Mariah starts to sweat a little thinking she probably saw her documentary or a recent picture since the police have probably found a little more evidence. Before she could even object the woman yells out "Some Of My Friends!" Mariah looks puzzled as the woman reminds her of a daily soap opera that comes on in the evening. She tells her that she looks like the mother which is one of the main characters. Mariah laughs to herself as a sign of relief and tells her that although the woman is not her, she wishes she could be. She tells her that she thinks acting is a wonderful career. The woman agrees and replies that it's too bad. She tells Mariah that she's just in time for the 3p.m. special. It means she gets a complimentary lunch with whatever room she picks. The two of them chat for another twenty minutes before she shows her where she will be staying. Good thing she doesn't judge a book by its cover. Maybe the front just needs a little updating because the room is literally to die for.

There's a king size bed, two fine dressers, two nightstands, a full kitchen area, a walk-in bathroom with a glass door and body length mirror, three fancy garbage cans, air fresheners, a huge television, and mints that spell out "enjoy your stay" across the bed. Mariah drops her stuff and makes herself right at home. Before hitting her head on the soft gray pillows that match the sheets   perfectly, she sees that the clock on the nightstand says 4:14p.m. Time is flying and she has to be ready in less than three hours to meet with Andrew. What to wear? How to do her hair?

She starts to over think patting her head and remembering that she shaved all of her hair off. Thank goodness for wigs, you could never go wrong with a little extra enhancement she thought as she modeled from the bed to the bathroom and back for approximately 15 minutes. After all of the back and forth and changing between jeans to shorts, skirts, dresses and hair lengths, she chooses to go just as she is. She decides to let him see her in her most natural state just as when he met her. She doesn't want to scare him away with only the second encounter. She wants to at least give him three dates before he really gets the chance to meet her. She's feels like that's been her biggest mistake for quite some time. She talks too much, she lets people in way too soon, and gives them more than they need to know about her. She's learning that people she's trusted have ran with valuable and descriptive information because she didn't leave enough room for mystery. So, with Andrew she swears things are going to be much different.

She's only looking for fun, a time that they can share and enjoy for that current moment. For the first time she isn't going to walk around with her heart or her sleeve expecting anything more than good company. She is tired of doing the same things and worse than getting the same results, her results are becoming added on headaches with each failed relationship whether it is personal, business, or most commonly family.

CHAPTER FIVE
Living Life With Andrew

Dear Diary,

I cried but only for a little because my mind already knew. It took my heart much longer but I was aware of what I had to do. Manipulated and Infatuated confused at the very least. Thinking it was love but love would never destroy my character nor disturb my inner peace. Lessening my value with each uncalled-for argument... Losing my head constantly stumbling in regret. I knew then what I know now. Lord knows I wish I didn't. I was never the one and your actions never hid it. Did everything in my power to force you to see me. But you're still gone without a trace we just weren't meant to be. Belittled, mocked, and ignored whatever way you could ridicule. Constantly felt like lessons but neither of us are still in school. Toughen up don't cry it's all for my good. I've been down this road before so I already understood. I asked for it because

I didn't follow every single rule. Has to always be your way otherwise you lose your cool. Can't speak my mind only talk when asked... Tell me I'm not smart poke fun and laugh. Now I'll be fair we had some good days or so I thought. But they wouldn't be complete unless we cursed and fought. Your ambition as a creator, your drive for success, your love for your family. These areas were your best. Could watch you for hours simply intrigued...

-Evelyn Beauvoir

It's been six months since Mariah and Andrew first met. It took just four dates and he begged her to leave the motel and move into his place with him over on Sagittarius Lane. It's one of the nicest streets in Pennsylvania. She didn't know at the time but Andrew isn't just a cashier. He owns the entire store. Once or twice a week he comes from out the back room hoping to meet new faces and see how they interact with everyone in the building regardless of the title. After he came clean to Mariah about his actual role, he told her that his mother taught him to treat people with the same respect. He said that the janitors and the cashiers are his equal. He said that every individual in is his eyes are equal and if people can't see that well then, he doesn't need their coins anyway. He told her that the store is his second home and his employees are his extended relatives. Finally, he told her that to him there is nothing more important than family. "You take care of home first and everything else after. If I'm good to my employees, I know my company will never fail because they will always feel the need to do their part. They will feel appreciated. One thing I've learned with any organization… yes customer service is definitely key. However, any person can wake up and decide another store is better. It can be for the simplest reason such as a shorter drive. As they go, with time other customers will come. But great employees are hard to come by. A solid team of dedicated individuals is like heaven on earth. If you have that team and the link weakens especially over something like being treated poorly…well that I cannot chance." Mariah is in awe hearing him speak the way he does. She's so used to money and greed being the driving force for people that she doesn't know how to accept such a soul like Andrew's. She wonders how can he be so modest. She wonders why wasn't he scared in losing money or how he can open his home to her so soon. She still has her guard up so she's been wondering why wouldn't he? He could see that without a doubt so he tries different approaches to show that everything he say, he means from the bottom of his heart. The same night that they met back at the super market he said that he could tell she was running from something, and that he hopes he were the best direction. He told her in any way that he can and that she feels most comfortable, he'd be there for her. She tried to question his gestures and he reiterated the fact that whatever she's done, whatever she's hiding from, that he is no better than she is. She tried to block out his words, his whole look said he was going to ruin her life. Really tall, nice build, tan, gray eyes, jet black colored hair…

beautiful indeed.

Over the course of the first two months the two were having a ball primarily focusing on a strong friendship. Back home the police are still struggling for clues as to what happened to her house. Reporters are all up and down Ashe Avenue talking to neighbors. They're not so eager to speak these days. Either way Mariah was in the clear, she wasn't a suspect. According to the different families everyone sided with Mariah's misfortune and still painted Elaine as the mastermind that led to so much turmoil. Karma's body was found during the third month but the signs of foul play made officials think she had a jealous ex-boyfriend. They also considered the woman from the front desk, but Mariah is again in the clear. Everyone that knew she and Mariah were related is already dead. She made sure of that.

She still hadn't heard from her parents, the twins didn't know about Karma, and it seemed like life was really beginning to turn around. The fourth month things were still pretty good. Andrew officially asked her to be his lady. He said once you're in your mid-thirties you can't be called a girlfriend. He said a woman like her deserved a far more sophisticated title. Although Mariah still wasn't over her past relationships, and she swore they all were different, she really thought Andrew had a certain spark that she couldn't deny. So, she said yes. She told him that they were already living and working together so why not. That's right her superb work ethic has helped her advance quickly in the store first as a cashier and then head of operations in just one month. All of the other employees are so happy for them.

They congratulated her saying things like *Andrew hasn't smiled like this ever*. He was always happy but this is a different happy. This is a **Mariah you make me better** kind of happy. She wasn't sure how to handle such positive feedback. One thing for sure, she loved it.

During alone time she'd sit in isolation and rearrange her thoughts. Although Andrew is wonderful, it's an inside job. He can't build her confidence... that is a job only she could perform. She thinks about her mother and how unintentionally she walked down a similar path. She still has her letters packed away. Sometimes she still reads them over trying to make her way into her mother's thoughts. She feels everything so deeply especially in regards to her mother. It made her think about her own conflicts and the sins she had to partake in to get where she is today. One day right in the middle of the fourth month while Andrew was away at the store, she started praying for forgiveness. She wasn't much of a religious woman, but it seemed to always work for her mama. Well, aside from spending a big chunk of her life behind bars. She began first by asking for forgiveness of her heinous acts. Then she asked God to forgive her for those that suffered the consequences, and lastly, she thanked God for Andrew. When she was all done, she stood back up from kneeling and went in the kitchen to prepare dinner. Andrew's shift was finishing up soon and she planned to surprise him with his favorite, mac and cheese, baked BBQ chicken, string beans, and corn. Mariah preferred friend chicken but she was trying to be healthier in picking her battles, so any chance she could she'd give Andrew his way. She worried more about the sides. She could taste the sweet corn and mac and cheese as if they were already in her mouth.

Unlike what she was used to growing up, Andrew continued to grow with the times. His house looked twice as up to date than even the updated version of her home you know before she burned it. There's a radio in the kitchen controlled by a remote. There's a tv screen that looks an inch or two bigger than a hand-held video game. She liked turning the volume up and down. She never got her own phone until she moved out of her parents' home. A cell phone was like a phenomenon. First, she learned that they record and things can be easily traced from them. In her dark line of work and secrets she never wanted that to happen. She didn't want to be listed in anyone's record. Think about it, she would have been found if she had a phone. Her team all either lived with or nearby and knew how to get in touch with her at all times. Although only 35-years-old, technology is a foreign language to her. But not as hard as it seems once she starts to get the hang of it. It's like once she got the dish washer down. Back home everything was done by hand. Her daddy tried his hardest to save a penny. That's where she got it from. That's where she went wrong. Andrew can't live without his gadgets. He just turned thirty but he's accustomed to a much different life than Mariah. He always has some type of an electronic nearby.

He says it's great that their parents and grandparents instilled the values of communication, spending time, and hard work however he enjoys his phone apps, media sites, and games just as much. In fact, that's probably one of their only arguments. Mariah once challenged Andrew to one whole evening without his phone, and he lost. He made multiple excuses like what if one of the employees tries to get in touch with him or a customer has a complaint. He's so hands on that the customer service number is attached to his personal line. All of the employees are given his number on the second day of work. He chooses the second day instead of the first to make sure they're really planning on coming back. He told her about a man that went missing the first day when he opened six years ago. He wanted to be a shift lead right then and there. When he didn't get his way not only did, he leave, but he put Andrews's number on three different websites and told the audience to call for a good time. Andrew didn't think it was a good time having to speak to hundreds of people explaining the altercation. Mariah didn't like that idea either way. She figured that incident should have changed his mind a long time ago. She told him where she was from things could have turned sour real quick. He just laughed and explained things only turn sour when people feel the need to justify or entertain them. He said he knew what he was and was not doing so it didn't make him a difference. He also told her did she always have to sound like she was born in 1960. She said no, but she should have been born then.

"Back when people had problems in Raleigh you either spoke to someone on shift during that time or kept making it a point to come back when the big boss was around. Customers rarely had to go so far as to call a number, and it definitely didn't connect to a home phone or personal line. Seems like you keeping the line clear for some other odd reason. I sure hope not," said Mariah. Andrew always talks right over those kinds of comments of hers. Mariah told him enough about her for him to know when she's getting ready for a rant. Instead he makes a clean exit by changing the subject to something. He only walked in the door 15 minutes ago and he could tell something is bothering her. After kicking his shoes off and leaving them on the small rectangular rug at the door, he sped straight to the kitchen where the smell of a fine home cooked meal opened up his pores and his heart. He lifts up the lid on each pan, and snatches a piece of skin from the chicken. As he raises his head Mariah pokes her head from out of the bathroom down the long hall. He blows her an air kiss and she blocks it.

"What's wrong now my little sour patch? Did you have a hard day off?" asked Andrew. "Nothing is wrong dear. How was your day today? Get any complaint calls today?" asked Mariah. "As a matter of fact I sure did not. What's that have to do with anything? Is everything okay? You've been a little out of it the past few days," said Andrew.

"Oh, you mean you've noticed something other than all your fancy gadgets? I feel honored. But no, I'm okay. Are you okay?" asked Mariah.

"I spot lots of things aside from my phone love. Like I notice you've been slightly moody. I don't know what you're thinking but I' m not them and you have nothing to worry about. Do you know how close we are to Philly and to everything else? It's damn near impossible to live as you do. I love you and I love what we have going on, but no one wants to live in isolation from the outside world at all times. It's like you're hiding from everything and everyone. As old as your soul is dear, you're not really that old. You should want to go out and get some fresh air. To be honest with you that goes for anyone regardless of their age. Two of my aunts still go out and have the time of their lives. Both are well into their 70's now. So. that's just you wanting to stay inside.

It's not your old spirit… *it's just you*," admitted Andrew. "If you say so. I don't really agree but for the prevention of a pointless argument I guess I'm making things more than they need to be. I won't go back and forth over things that should be addressed. We will do it your way dear," replied Mariah.

"Now here you go, that's not what I meant and you know it. I just want you to feel comfortable that's all. I've been working on something for you for about two weeks or so. I know I've been suspicious but I can promise it's all with good intentions," said Andrew

"Really? And what would you be working so diligently on?" asked Mariah. "Here, listen to the last voicemail and tell me who it sounds like," said Andrew.

"Is that Melody or Melissa," asked Mariah.

"It's actually both of them. Melody was speaking first and Melissa concluded. You're living in a bubble however they've adapted to technology so I see. I was able to locate Melody on a social networking site for business leaders. She has quite the following… 400,000 and only 10,000 in which she follows back. Not to mention lots of awesome family and travel visuals. Do you know she recently visited Egypt and Asia to host a seminar? She's quite impressive if I do say so myself. She's almost a little intimidating. But I took a chance in contacting her. I liked three travel photos before respectfully commenting underneath a family one. To my surprise she replied back within the same hour. I was stoked. Like what made me stand out? Anyway, I made my case straight to the point. I told her how we've been seeing each other. I told her I thought it would be a great idea if she and Melissa were able to visit. I told her I felt like you were feeling down or doubting me and that I really wanted to do something special for you. For some odd reason she didn't believe that you and I were involved. She said you all didn't know anything about Pennsylvania and that it seemed weird you would land here. Then she asked if I spoke to Melissa yet and I told her no but I planned to. She said she was totally here for it and wanted Melissa to know just as much as she does. She started to ask more about my profession, my credit, education, family, and if I had any sort of record. I think that was the exam. Once I gave the acceptable answers, she said she'd be delighted in surprising you and arranged for the three of us to have a phone conference. That was the next step. Melissa is more relaxed, she's like a mixture of you and Melody. She's a lady boss for sure, but she doesn't need the public attention. She has two separate accounts, one for business and the other is strictly for friends and family. I was unable to see any of the children, her spouse, or anything not pertaining to her company. But what I learned during our phone conference, is that they're both full time mothers and married now amongst various other things. Melody's husband owns multiple car dealerships, and Melissa and Her husband are partners. They own a chain of Daycares called First Lyrics Child Development Center. Her husband is a former poet and wanted to add an artistic touch. Did you know any of this? You know they're both married? They spoke as if you all have been out of touch for a while," said Andrew.

"Wow, I'm not sure whether to smile or scream. You've been snooping around my backyard? What made you so curious? Why didn't you ask me to tell you a little more about them before going on a full-blown search? You don't think it's a little strange? It's okay to be inquisitive but this seems much more like prying and sticking your nose where it doesn't belong. We've been living together but if I'm being honest, I'm already interrogating you so how do you know I really set my heart on you all meeting," asked Mariah.

"Well there you have it. I thought you were acting distant with me and I figured speaking with those that know you best would help. I wasn't trying to upset you nor be sneaky. But it's great that the truth comes out when you're mad." Mariah sucks her teeth and walks down the hall to use the bathroom. When she closes the door, she hears Andrew speaking with someone. He sounds annoyed, telling them that he can't seem to get it right no matter what he does. She starts snickering to herself thinking how she can accuse him of prying and she's doing the same exact thing. Their bathroom looks like it belongs to a famous movie star or a celebrity. She normally leaves her lady products underneath the sink. Where she's seated on the toilet to the cabinet is in reaching distance so she normally doesn't have to do much movement at all. She slides up to reach inside to grab something when Andrew's voice suddenly becomes a whisper. She doesn't think too much of it, but she hurries along washing her hands and face before twisting the doorknob. She takes a step forward and the tile creaks. Like a magic trick the cabinet opens back up. She walks over to close it and bumps her head on her way back up on their mirror cabinet. The magic trick traveled and that one opened up too.

She never had a reason to look in it. Andrew calls it his personal pharmacy away from the aisle at the store. He's a firm believer in representing the brands of the company, so he has both the name and generic brands right in his cabinet. Mariah never had to go in prior to this second because luckily neither of them have gotten sick since dating. Andrew gains a voice again and yells out if she's okay. She yells back of course, that her stomach is upset and that she's looking for something to put her hair up away from her face.

She has a bin full of clips, combs, curlers and things so it could take a little while. While she's continuing to look over things, she yells out a gut-wrenching scream and says she caught a terrible cramp. She thinks that will buy her at least ten to fifteen more minutes. She's lactose, but she loves cheese. Andrew has tried time and time again to convince her of letting go of dairy but she just won't. And on top of that she refuses to take anything for it or any kind of substitutes. She always tells him back in her day she'd eat an ice cream or two, make her way to the ladies' room, go about her day, and twenty minutes want another ice cream. She said that was when she didn't really worry because the pains only lasted long enough for her to order the desert. She said that's the worst part about growing up. She said her stomach although flat as an ironing board, is pretty crappy when considering her digestive system. Almost anything that goes in, comes right back out. Andrew's voice gets much louder.

The phone conversation sounds different, his tone changes drastically. He's laughing and everything. Mariah starts to wonder what's going on out there, but continues looking through the medicine. She finds a whole bunch of nothing aside from pain relievers and cough syrup. What a crock she thinks to herself. At the same time, she walks over to flush the toilet once more, Andrew comes tapping at the door. He says a client just called and asked him to meet at the store right this minute. Mariah waits before responding and he assures her she has nothing to worry about. He tells her he's a man from Connecticut just passing through. He wants to do some collaborating before he gets to his final destination. He says the store just happened to be along the trail. Mariah says okay, Andrew makes a squishy kissing noise, grabs his briefcase and heads out the door. Mariah still isn't convinced. She tears the bathroom a part. She lifts up the tiles, scratches at the walls, slides the ceiling tiles, removes the top of the toilet, sits in the bathtub for a break, and still she finds nothing. Then it dawns on her that maybe there is something to find but it's not in the bathroom. She thinks maybe he's a little smarter than he looks. *Maybe she's assuming.* Is Andrew really different from everyone else? Does he really want her and her sisters to rekindle their relationship without any hidden motive?

She walks out the bathroom and heads into the bedroom. She sits on her side of the bed for a brief rest. She tries to let her urge go, but she doesn't have it in her. She knows there's something she's overlooking. Her destructive pursuit makes the rooms look almost identical to one another. She starts remembering all of her therapy notes. She tries to think practically, but she's still puzzled about Andrew's curiosity. There's nothing where they sleep either aside from their roomy bed, matching rug, wooden drawers and the closet full of clothes that she threw everywhere. She grabs a sweater she hadn't worn in a while put it on and headed for the living room. You could say she's still pretty adamant. Andrew is such a neat freak it's ridiculous. There's no way she could move anything without him knowing. Then again at this point she didn't care much about him knowing anything. He was already going to have an attack about the first two rooms so why not conclude with a bang she thought. She picks up the olive-green pillow on the loveseat and sees a copy of 'PUR3 SPIRIT' Magazine. She takes a break to catch up on the latest gossip. It actually calms her down. Then out of nowhere she hears Andrew's phone. She thinks that can't be possible she knows he left already and she also knows he took all his devices with him. He never leaves home without them. It won't stop ringing; the person is calling back to back. Just as soon as it stops it starts back up again.

She walks over to the marble kitchen countertop where the phone is placed next to a sticky note of dates and names. She ignores the note for now and turns her attention totally onto the phone. It looks like Andrew's, it's the same model for certain, but it has scratches at the bottom as if it fell a couple times. Mariah picks it up and looks at it. She's not so sure how to work it but she does see a button that says answer. The caller ID says unknown however as soon as the person speaks, she knows for sure who it is. It's a woman that she didn't think she'd hear from again nor did she think she'd find a way to contact Andrew.

She gets really quiet, goes in the refrigerator to grab a bottle of wine, and leans against the counter. Out loud she thinks to herself what a day. The voice laughs and agrees, telling her it's just getting started. She tells Mariah that she has a choice between two scenarios. She explains that if Mariah chooses not to do as she says, she will immediately call the police and give them every piece of evidence they need to keep her in prison until she reaches heaven or hell in her case. Mariah tells the voice to calm her temper that her attitude isn't needed and she's open to considering the options. She tells her if she finds them to be up to par then maybe they'll have a more to converse over. She also says if she doesn't, that she's never scared to suffer any consequence and that she better be sure whatever she thinks she has will stick for her own good. The voice tells her she has enough to stick her and everyone else around her.

Mariah sarcastically cackles and says that before she's given the options she'd like to know about her involvement with Andrew, why he has more than one phone and if she knows details about him reaching out to the twins. The woman tells her that she and Andrew have been seeing each other for two years. Mariah says in a deep voice that can't be since she and Andrew have been dating for almost six months now. The voice laughingly says she knows, and the entire time she's had the chance to keep tabs on everything that they do. She tells her it's by no accident that Andrew found her. Mariah tries to bring up various accounts and the voice tells her even from the first moment at the grocery store, that everything was an act; he already knew who she was. Mariah tries to find a way to justify him knowing of her by pointing out the fire and the local news station and the voice follows up with a rebuttal. She asked her if she ever heard of James Dexter before. Mariah said no but assumed he's a new reporter just starting out in the field. She told her it's uncommon to know every news personality. She told her what kind of loser actually watches the news enough to know how long someone has been with the company and whether or not they have actual credentials. The voice replied a loser that's trying not to serve a life sentence in jail. This is why it's smart to be cautious. James Dexter is Andrew's best friend. He actually owns a construction company. Mariah feels herself becoming faint so she sits down on the arm of the chair back in the den. The voice tells her that everything will be okay if she makes the right choice. She tells her that she knew things wouldn't work between them and that she had no choice in covering her tracks because if she hadn't, she would be six feet under like everyone else. Mariah told her that wasn't the case that she didn't mean for things to go the way they did but she is just protective of herself since clearly, she has no one else. She asked her who would allow Dexter and Andrew to fabricate evidence and play on tv. The voice responded probably the same person that allowed you and Justyce McCall. Mariah saw that one coming so she didn't throw a punch back. Instead she asked if Andrew needing to leave was a part of everything. The voice responded oh but of course, and that she needed for them to speak privately so that Mariah understands it's personal. Then she told her if the survey is over, she'd like to continue with the selections. She said option number one is to turn herself in completely. Back home they're still looking for hints and clues all of which she has with her. She says that if she likes she can tell the truth, the proof will be delivered, but her conscious will be free. Mariah says interesting and inquiries about option number two. The voice responds by saying she always wanted to be a hero in some sort of way. Mariah tells her she doesn't think she's following and the voice tells her don't play ignorant that she knows exactly what she means. She tells Mariah that she'd like to appear as the person that captured her. She explains to Mariah that since she beat the curse once she'd be likely to beat it again if she pleads temporary insanity a second time. She says it would make sense as to why she snapped and killed everyone in the house fire. Mariah starts laughing hysterically. The woman over the phone is not amused at all. "So, my first choice is to be a totally honest woman about everything that happened. And my second choice is to be honest except without including your actual role but instead give you the identity of some sort of super woman. Am I understanding you correctly?" asked Mariah.

"Yes, that's correct. I thought we had a deal but you showed me that I was being oblivious to the fact that the only person Mariah Beauvoir is concerned with helping…is herself. You want to be the victim so bad, and at first you were. But you turned everything around in a negative way and you have become a monster. The entire time I was only trying to help. You tricked me causing me to go against my better judgment. You owe this to me in order to really make things right."

"*Do I have donkey written across my face?* Seriously how do I benefit from any of this? And let's be clear sister, I didn't put a gun to your head. You wanted to prove you could keep up with the big dogs. As far as I'm concerned Karma was bound to come your way," said Mariah.

"You can laugh now, but I'll laugh later. You're right you didn't put a weapon to my head. But you did to Rebecca Townsend. What about Justyce and Joey? They struggled before that fire. Your prints were on everything in the house. Did you stick around long enough to make sure it burned all the way down? Let me answer for you... you sure did not. Otherwise I wouldn't have what I have. See if you let Joey live a little longer, you'd have him around to dig you out of the pile of *dookey* you just stepped in. Looks like this time things won't be so easy. You know I didn't even think to ask you where are you going to stay now? I know you probably don't want to continue living at Andrew's knowing I picked out those silky turquoise sheets, the rug that your feet touch when you get up to open the matching turquoise curtains. I didn't get to change them yet this week, my favorite are the gold ones. I've never seen any like them before. Word on the street I hear you like them too," said Karma.

"What is wrong with you? Do you think you're Elaine? What are you trying to do here? Wait, do you think you're me? You're sick. You can't outsmart me. This is my skit. Stay in your place!" yelled Mariah. "Oh gosh... my feelings are almost hurt. That was really mean. But at least I'm not sicker than you. I don't need Andrew unlike you. I really don't want him either. He was just a source of help. Plus, I barely know you psycho. Don't flatter yourself. I'd die before I walk in your desperate steps. Then again you tried that and you couldn't even follow through so how smart are you? I'm not dead Mariah. You couldn't pull that one off," said Karma.

"It sounds good, but I know a lie when I hear it. So, fame and money is all you're seeking? I didn't even get a dime yet. You know that. Before the incident with you we were a team," said Mariah.

"Spare me the mind game. I'm not the one. I know you didn't get anything yet, but you're going to. Right? That's why you went so far? There has to be a big lump to make you risk your freedom again. Then again who knows? You do lack common sense," said Karma.

"You're right hopefully I will soon. It should be a whole lot if I'm not mistaken. I can't transfer anything. Although it's been a few months I still don't want to look suspicious. It's $100,000 we're talking about here. Plus, that $20,000 I found on you. Oh yeah you never did mention that. But since we're talking common sense, why would I leave anything to you and not my twin sisters that I've known my entire life? Who do you think is going to believe that? Who will believe you? Who even knows you? No one knows who you are," said Mariah.

"It's a shame, so much potential gone to waste. Come on work with me. I'm really starting to think Joey killed Elaine all by himself. You really don't seem so capable. Our twin sisters have been working with Andrew and I. They found out about Andrew right after you fake killed me. But we've been running a separate show since before you and I left Raleigh. Who do you think went back for my special evidence once we left? I know I know it's a lot to take in. Don't stop breathing on me," said Karma.

"You're a liar. I know what you're trying to do but it won't work. They're my siblings not yours. They would never," said Mariah. "How sure are you? I bet you wouldn't bet your life on it. What are the odds all of a sudden Andrew is in contact with both and you all are going to be one big happy family? Yes, a lot is true they are incredibly successful, married, and mother's but who wouldn't enjoy more money and the chance to put a nag like you away once and for all? I have the answer again; would you like to hear it?" asked Karma. "You're disgruntled because of our father and your mother. That wasn't and still isn't my fault," said Mariah.

"Ahh that's a nice vocabulary word. I'll be sure to use it during my first live interview. Don't worry sister I'll give you credit. In such a short period of time you inspired me. How does that sound? Oh, my goodness the public is going to eat it up. I can see it now Morgan Karma Garcia the half-sister that loved whole heartedly. Wow that almost sounds like a movie even. Hey maybe I can get an honest Journalist. I don't know where you found yours," said Karma.

"It almost sounds identical to my plan. Looks like you found a way to cut me out. If the twins would do something like this to me, what makes you think they won't stab you too," asked Mariah?

"They had to live their entire lives hearing you cry and nag about Dad and everything else. Then they watched you flip it to your advantage and get away with murder literally multiple times while they actually made a career for themselves. Oh yes, I know because I've been around much longer than I led you to believe. See what being a narcissistic prick gets you? You've been living your fantasy for so long that you didn't even see actual reality happening. I'll leave it at this, I'm not worried about anyone or anything. The only one that should be worried dear... *is you*. Now before I let you go tend to making dinner because I'm sure that was your original plan for this beautiful evening...I want to leave you with my final thought until we speak again. Oh yes, I'll be in touch so you can let me know which option you've decided. Nevertheless, do us all a favor and don't try anything funny. You are already aware of how skeptical I am of you. Try not to add on please. I would hate to take everything into my own hands without hearing your decision, but if I must I will. Are we clear sister?" asked Karma.

"As clear can be... sister," said Mariah.

"Stupendous! Okay, well I hope you enjoy the remainder of your day. Andrew should be back momentarily. If you need me sooner than expected, he knows how to reach me. Love you, I'll talk to you soon," said Karma.

CHAPTER SIX
You Can't Run From Karma

As soon as Mariah and Karma hang up the phone Andrew comes prancing back in through the door as if he was on cue and nothing ever happened. He sees Mariah holding the phone and starts to grin. She's standing with her right hand placed on her hip, lips poked out, and her left hand balled up in a fist. She blinks twice, takes a big gulp, and tells him to shut up. Andrew's grin runs away as his eyes grow bigger taking up most of the room on his face. Then he bravely moves closer to her. Mariah steps back warning him that if he moved again it would be the last thing he did. Then she shows him the phone. As Andrew looks through, he's confused. All it shows is a recent call from a number with no ID. She tells him to cut the act, that he knows exactly who called her. Andrew is puzzled. He thought he was doing the right thing in trying to bring her up to speed with technology. He wanted her to try it out and see if she likes it. He's not so sure what feature or app confused her but no one should have called her. Mariah is sure that he is lying to her. She tells him to confess about knowing and having a relationship with Karma. She also tells him that she knows the twins are in on everything. Andrew's sitting on the sofa with his shoes kicked off and scratching his temple. Every time he tries to butt in, she tells him to shut up, that everything is a lie and she doesn't want to hear it. She starts name calling and using language that she normally wouldn't.

Finally, Andrew can't take it anymore.

He decides to get up from the seat and walk back toward her. She warns again that he's getting too close and he says he knows and doesn't care because he loves her so it's worth the risk of losing a body part. Then he explains that of course he knows the twins. They discussed this before he left. He tells her they are coming to visit but there is no funny business going on.

He tells her that he doesn't know anything about anyone named Karma. She didn't talk much about her relationships with others so he really isn't so sure where all of this is coming from. She's starting to cool down, well she dropped her fist at least. He hugs her tight and tells her that whatever is aggravating her, they will get through together. He tells her the last thing he ever wants to do is lose her trust. He says the twins are coming as a way to make her feel more at home and to open up, but if she's not up for it he could kindly tell them never mind. Mariah is quietly sitting in the kitchen with one hand on her lap and the other pressed against her face. She's still trying to understand the call. She tells him that whoever called if not Karma herself, they knew too much about things she only discussed with her. She tells him that she isn't disturbed, that someone is playing a game then. Andrew gives her a look of concern because he is aware that she spent some time in a center. Mariah catches it quick and tells him not to think about it. She says that she knows what's imagined and what reality is. She says it even shows in her call log that someone called so it's evident that she's not making it up. Andrew calms his tone as a way to reassure her but feels something is really wrong. He's not sure of what transpired while he was away but he has no clue about any of her accusations.

Mariah can sense he doesn't believe her so she goes back to the call. She shows him again to show the amount of time. He nods his head and says it's clear that she spoke with someone but he's still not sure exactly who. Mariah starts to cry out of exasperation. She puts her head down in her lap and starts rocking back and forth. Andrew leans down and lifts her chin up. He tells her it's okay and that she doesn't have to cry. He tells her that whatever she did or didn't do, he loves her. Mariah instantly snatches her tears and looks him dead in the eye. He repeats himself and says that whoever she spoke with has saddened her. He assumes that this person knows something about her that she's not ready to share with anyone else, so he wants her to know should the person come out of hiding and or anything decides to come knocking at their door, that he's down for the long run. As he pulls her back in again for a warm embrace, he compliments her perfume and her hair. He tells her that everything will be fine and heads into their room to freshen up before dinner. Mariah nods, twirls her hair a little and grabs a banana and bottle of water from the refrigerator. She desperately wants to believe him but it's not like she hasn't heard the same speech before... *it's déjà vu.*

As she closes the fridge back, she slams it a little hard. As many times as Andrew tells her to be gentle, she's slightly heavy handed so it always sounds like a car crash. Andrew hears it and jokingly says "Well I guess your hands still haven't gotten any lighter yet..." She yells out, "...you guessed it babe!" and immediately after, the shower turns on. A small piece of yellow paper floats in front of her sneakers. It looks like it could have fallen from the impact of the bang. She bends down to pick it up. When she reads the message, she nearly drops her whole water on the floor. The shower is still running, Andrew normally stays in there longer than she does. He told her when they first began dating that he still measures his level of cleanliness by how wrinkly he could make his skin. Sounds a little childish, but he always smells like heaven on earth. Especially if it's a gym day or he does an extra shift on the register at work. He'll take two or more showers. He told Mariah it's a habit since he was a boy. One day while still in elementary school another boy tried to be entertaining in front of everyone on the playground by making fun of his hygiene. At the time Andrew was so young he couldn't even say if it were true or not. He went home and cried to his mother. She consoled him and told him that sometimes kids say things without knowing the actual meaning behind their words. She promised him he'd never hear it again, and he never did. Too bad stigma was already there. Mariah knew because of this she had much more time to investigate than the average person would. The message read **"YOU'RE NOT CRAZY... CHECK HIS PHONE."** Normally, Mariah would never because aside from knowing nothing about it, Andrew has yet to make her second guess their relationship. She didn't want to keep living the same experiences. But that's until now. He always leaves his phone hanging around because he knows she pays it no mind. She looks in the living room but it's nowhere to be found. She checks all over the kitchen trying to trace their steps and remember the last time he had it in his hand. She can't think... she starts telling herself to remember when, where in the house was, he. Then it comes to her. He had it in his pocket. It was never in his hand which means it's either in the bathroom with him or somewhere in their room. She couldn't imagine it be anywhere near water with the possible risk of water damage. So, she yells out honey are you wrinkled yet to get a reply before checking his side of the room. It isn't much of a search at all. As soon as she walks in the room right by the nightstand is his phone all lit up. Looks like someone either sent a message or a call just now. Mariah gets as close as she possibly can to the phone. As soon as she places her right hand on the nightstand in attempt to grab it, the shower water stops running and she hears Andrew's footsteps coming her way.

She pulls her hand back and quickly hops on the bed. On her side she has a short book shelf filled with magazines and other sorts of stories. She yanks one out, opens it up, kicks her shoes off and starts speaking out loud as Andrew excitedly comes in talking. He says it looks like she's feeling much better. The selection in her hand is titled TWELVE. It's a book of poetry, reflections, and fictional scenarios. She's read it many times so Andrew says that really must be your favorite. She responds sarcastically saying yes, that she's on one of the poems that acknowledges self –worth. Andrew takes the shade with pride and sits down on the bed beside her with his bottle of cocoa butter lotion. She tells him to scoot over just a smidge. She tells him she can't breathe past his fragrance. His eyebrows scrunch really close together and he says fine, gets up completely off the bed, and walks back into the bathroom. He yells out of annoyance, how about he just continue getting himself together and he'll return once the scent dies a little. He thought she was being wise because he knows he told her about elementary school and he knows his lotion smells remarkable. Mariah let out a phony laugh and agreed that would be best so she could make her way back to the sketchy telephone of his. She still has the book in her left hand, and with her right she swipes the phone and places it behind the cover to give the illusion that she's still reading. She goes to the recent calls not knowing where to start, but she sees that one number keeps calling and has been calling nonstop for almost two weeks in a row.

Before deciding whether or not to call, she thinks of all the possibilities, like what if it's just a childhood buddy, or what if it's a work buddy. Then she contemplates another direction and considers that it could be a business investor. She thinks what if it's taking a little longer than usual to seal the deal. Then she finally thinks what most men think women assume from the very beginning…what if it's another woman? But in her case even more disgusting, what if it's another woman and that other woman is her newfound sister? She thinks what if Karma was right and Andrew has a hidden agenda? What if he's working with her sisters? She getting all worked up so she stops trying to guess and hits the button to dial the number. As the voice that belongs to a woman says hello, Andrew walks in the room looking for his phone. Luckily, Mariah tosses it but unfortunately, she didn't get to delete it from his log. "Well how did that get all the way over there? I thought I left it by my watch on the nightstand. Well I have been rushing around trying to care for my skin without being in someone's way," said Andrew.

"Exactly dear you probably tossed it without even knowing where it landed. So, what are you getting ready to do now? How is the store, should I go in for a few hours? I can shower and head over if you like," said Mariah.

"I have a conference with two gentlemen from Montana. They flew in yesterday. They think I have great potential and they're looking to expand in marketing. If I win them over, they're willing to invest in us and open up ten more stores all over," said Andrew. "Are they now? Dear that's excellent. And I'm sorry what are their names? I don't think you mentioned before," said Mariah "Oh yes, Harrison and Hank. They're actually cousins," said Andrew.

"Ah I see how convenient… I mean how great is that? Well I know you're going to knock them dead babe. I'm super proud of you."

"Aw honey, that's super loving of you. I needed that. See, when you're not insinuating preposterous things look at how sweet you can actually be. Now this is my golden girl right here. This is why I love you," said Andrew.

"I do try love, I'm glad you can tell," said Mariah. Andrew got dressed, made his conference, landed the investors, and he and Mariah celebrated that weekend. In fact, they extended the weekend and celebrated for an extra three days the following week. Andrew had some of the most trustworthy employees take over while he and Mariah enjoyed a romantic winter getaway in Puerto Rico. While there, they learned so much more about each other. For example, Andrew had no clue that she's fluent in Spanish and he also didn't know about her fear of swimming until she almost drowned. Mariah learned that she could count on Andrew at least long enough not to let her sink to the bottom of the ocean. He came to her rescue rather quickly. Once they returned home to Pennsylvania Andrew made sure to be at work first thing in the morning. Mariah had different plans. She was sitting on the couch double checking her bag to make sure that she had everything she needed. While Andrew started as a fun time and even turned into a good guy, she never did solve the mystery about his phone and she wasn't going to continue being involved with someone that may or may not be trying to set her up. The trip was a nice distraction but she still had her mind set on the prize. The random number slowed down, and she hasn't heard anything else yet from Karma, but she's no fool. Before they left for the trip, she tried to get in contact with both of the twins. Coincidentally each of their numbers are no longer in service. She thought just as soon as she tried to start picking up some of the technology, there it went failing her. If they could have vouched for Andrew maybe things could be different but since they couldn't be tracked, he still looked sketchy. So, this is the best idea she could come up with. She's all cried out from everyone else that she doesn't have any to give to Andrew. Here's to Good-bye.

My Dearest Andrew Addison,

I'm really happy that I had the blessing in being acquainted with you. Who would have ever thought seeing you in the grocery store just some months ago would have led us to where we are today? April will always be my favorite month because of you. I know I also didn't think you'd own the store at such a young age nor did I think I'd date a full-blown white man. Okay that part I did. I've had jungle fever forever but the guys that I've dated have always been mixed with a little something, you know sort of like me. Anyway, that doesn't matter if you were blue, green, brown, beige or white, I'd choose you again and again. I want to think that we could live happily ever after. To be truthful I did think that until two weeks ago. It's just not sitting well with me. There's something in your phone and something attached to that random decoy phone you disguised as a gift. I actually misplaced it too. I apologize about that. See I've been so busy trying to keep up with yours and playing Officer Beauvoir, that I'm losing sight of everything else around me. No one deserves to live like that. No relationship can prosper on these terms. Since I met you, we have been growing as a unit, but somewhere between me moving in and the suspicious call, something happened. I thought once I find out what you're keeping from me maybe we could move on. But I've been watching you. You don't think anything is wrong. In fact, you let the conversation go and you haven't brought it up again since. So, then it leads me to think am I making things more, or is there more that you're keeping and I just haven't stumbled hard enough yet. Maybe there is a time and place for what you're hiding. I just didn't get to make it there in time. However, I don't plan on waiting any longer. I've learned a lot from you and I won't forget the great times we've had but I think someone that knows the old me is trying to pay me a visit. I don't want you or anyone else to get hit by my karma.

-Mariah S. Beauvoir

As Mariah folds the letter into the perfect rectangle, she slowly places it on the kitchen table. Then she grabs one last juice box and the sandwich baggie of grapes and puts them next to her purse and bags. She's not sure how long it'll take her to get back to Raleigh so she needs to use the bathroom before getting back on the road. While gathering tissue she notices the sink which is where she keeps all her hair products. Andrew is always telling her to put the curlers and things away because he's such a neat freak. She just never listened. Today is no different aside from the fact that it's a few items short of the regular count and the comb and brush are spread out. Mariah breaks down wishing things could be different tossing her products from one end of the sink to the other when all of a sudden, she sees a blue bobby pin that doesn't belong to her. Not only is it blue, but it's customized and she knows exactly who the owner is.

An ocean flows down her face as the wind knocks the blinds back and forth against the bathroom window. Her legs shake unsteady like a wobbly table, and her hands turn cold and hard. She hurries up in the bathroom and gets her bags. On the table while looking at the letter one last time, she catches a glimpse of a pile of mail. Her mind tells her to look, so she listens. The third sealed envelope from the top is sent from Ashe Avenue in Raleigh. Her heart jumps out of her chest. She replays everything she and Andrew talked about, but nothing is clicking. But she knows she's right, there's no doubt about it. Why else would he have a letter from her old address when he lives all the way out here in Pennsylvania and knows nothing about her town at all? Her mind is jumping hurdles, but she knows time is ticking and she needs to get out before something else happens. She puts the mail back exactly how she found it and runs to the door. She grabs the door and quickly turns it. Instead of looking at what's in front of her, her neck is turned still locked on the table causing her to miss the force getting ready to strike her. Two blows to the head, and one to the legs. Her body instantly collapses and hits the ground. The impact is so strong that the pictures that were lined up against the wall fall and the glass shatters all over creating an ear-piercing sound.

CHAPTER SEVEN
Have A Safe Stay

*"Hello, welcome to **Safe Stay Psychiatric Center** where we guarantee a warm, loving, and healthy environment today and every day....*

How can I help you?"

"Hmm right, is this 9012 Wilkey Way Plaza? My name is Elaine Townsend. I'm looking for Mariah Beauvoir. Is she here? I was informed earlier this week that she had another episode and things got a little ugly. Most times the doctors are able to control her but I'm guessing this time is was really bad. That's the reason for the sudden transfer I'm sure. You know everyone has their level of tolerance. But I'm here to see her," said Elaine. "Oh, I see. Are you her mother?"

"Close, I'm her aunt. I'm actually her favorite aunt just don't let her tell it," answered Elaine.

"Oh, how awesome is that? Close knit families are great. Yes… she is here right in the recreation room. And I didn't really think you were her mother. You actually look about her age."

"Yeah, she's almost 36 now. As for I well you know what they say…black don't crack. Can't tell you my age because that would be impolite of me. But I'm blessed for sure," said Elaine.

"Oh, ok well that's not a problem. But I do need to see your license. I promise not to look at the age. Is anyone else going to be accompanying you?" "Alright, I guess that's fine. You can see it. And no child it's just me. My husband is home and our daughter Rebecca is long gone off living her life in Pennsylvania. She attended college at Cheyney University for business. While there she met a young man named Andrew Addison. He's originally from Philadelphia Pennsylvania. She said he won her over because his heart is pure and filled with love. She also said he looked like one of the tall hunky white surfer boys from California… whatever that means. His mama is black, and his daddy was white but he didn't get a lick of her color not that she had much to spare. Rebecca said at College the only way they knew he had a little something in him was when he decided to pledge. He moves like you never seen before. When I saw the videos on those media sites you kids use today, I said oh yeah, he's the one. After she finished her final semester, he told her if she moved out that way that they'd take over the grocery store market and really have the chance to put their degrees to work. His daddy was business savvy. He taught him everything he know. It's only a little over five years now and they're married with a set of twins. One of each, a little boy and a little girl named Michael and Michelle. His dad's name was Michael and they thought Michelle fit perfectly for the girl. On top of that he is indeed a man of his word. They own twelve stores spread throughout the states. Two of them in Pennsylvania, and one actually about five miles up the road. They have a shore house in New Jersey and everything," said Elaine.

"Now isn't that just lovely. I swear I love hearing about good homes. I mean I know Mariah must have gone through somethings to be here but it's wonderful she has family like you all… you know it gives her hope maybe one day she can venture off like your daughter did"

"That's surely nice of you to say such a thing. I'm guessing you're new… *Ms. MK Garcia is it?*" asked Elaine.

"Oh, I apologize how rude of me. Yes, my name is quite long. It's Morgan Karma Garcia. The patients all call me Karma." "That's a beautiful name. How long have you been working here? You don't seem so familiar with my niece. I know she's only been in this facility temporarily but everybody from Virginia to Georgia knows about Mariah probably even more by now," said Elaine. "I guess you got me huh? I haven't lived out this way for too long. I'm from Brooklyn, New York. My brother Joey has lived down here forever. I'm not totally up to date with Mariah's case but I do know of her. Joey actually went to high school with her. He's asked about her since she's been here. He invited me a few summers ago to one of his networking events. I put up a fight, but in the end, I was actually glad I went because I met so many wonderful people like Justyce McCall," said Morgan.

"Oh my gosh you mean the Journalist from the Nightly Show," asked Elaine. "The one and only. He's super cool. We actually watch him on television here sometimes," replied Elaine.

"That's so funny, they watch him at the old facility too. Mariah is borderline obsessed with him. They actually attended high school together too. Yeah, they were great friends until well you know," said Elaine. "Actually, I would like to know more. I mean I've looked at her chart but maybe everything hasn't been filled out just yet. Why is she here? Did she do something? I've never even heard her speak to anyone except the Mendez sisters. It's strange, when she got here, they both came with her. The supervisor said there would be no way in holding her without them. She said Mariah calls them her sisters, that she calls them the twins," said Morgan.

"Oh yes the Mendez sisters. They're so sweet. As little girls me, Evelyn, their mother and their aunt attended Sunday school together. We felt much happier when we found out they'd be with Mariah. Once she recognized their familiar faces, she became happy for some time. They're adults now too, but I'll always look at them as little girls. I can't believe they're nurses. Anyway, Mariah was a little over 15 years old, when the incident occurred. You see as a little girl my sister and her father did their best in giving her whatever she wanted. Mariah never knew the word no. Discipline just wasn't a thing. Now it's not like she was a bad kid, because she wasn't for the most part, she needed more structure but nothing so detrimental or so we thought. She wanted siblings, but after my sister had her she suffered two miscarriages and later was told it would be impossible to have another child," said Elaine.

"*Wait so she is an only child?*" asked Morgan.

"Yes and no. Her father has children outside of his relationship with her mother," said Elaine.

"Oh, I see," said Morgan. "Sometimes marriages don't work out, I'm sure we're all aware of that as women but when you're a seven year old child and you walk in on Daddy with a woman other than Mommy, it can be triple as painful," said Elaine. "Oh, my lord, poor child," said Morgan.

"That's when things started little by little. There were small lies she'd go to school and tell her teachers. She'd blame things on the twins and question her father's love. The only twins were the Mendez girls. They've been friends forever but, in her mind, they were her siblings. We thought maybe the sisters she always wanted but couldn't have. In middle school she couldn't deal with my sister working so much. Things aren't like they are today. It was the 90's and technology wasn't as advanced so sometimes her schedule would conflict. So, as a way to gain more of her mother's attention, she'd tell my sister that her father was mistreating her. He never treated her different. There wasn't anyone to compare treatment with. His other children lived way up north. Mariah has never even met her other siblings. His mother and his sister Spark never spoke ill of her either. Spark has been married Mariah's entire life. She lives in Texas, and has four grown boys with her husband. Their mother passed away from natural causes four years ago. Yup she was still alive that whole time. You see what the mind can do when the heart is broken? I hope you don't think any different of my niece. She's still a human. She made mistakes, but she needed help long before her 15th birthday. Had her mama listened to her cries maybe there would have been a better chance in saving the both of them," said Elaine.

"The both of them? So how far did she go? Who exactly did she harm to end up here like this?" asked Morgan. "Well child she ain't all mixed up. The notes she writes all day long is a combination of her own thoughts and thoughts she read from her mama. She found out that my sister wasn't so innocent and blind to what her daddy was doing. Her mama was cheating too. And she couldn't have more kids not because of miscarriages, but because of two abortions. She wasn't sure if they belonged to Mariah's father so she did what she thought was best...and so did Mariah," said Elaine. "Wait what was best? What did she do?" asked Morgan.

"It was a cold stormy Halloween in October. The girls were teens now so they didn't do much dressing up you know. Rebecca was there, my husband, Mariah, and her parents. Everyone was having a good time. Whatever issues my sister had going on in her marriage, they weren't showing at all that night. Just a whole lot of positivity and love going around, you know? Not for long... we were in the living room playing scrabble and listening to WBLS when the power went out. Everyone was annoyed, but it's no surprise Carolina storms known to pack a punch. None of us noticed, but throughout the night Mariah was constantly watching me and her uncle, and Rebecca. I know, it sounds more envious, but she wasn't. She was admiring us to be what she believed a real family should be. I wish then I could have held her and told her how much Rebecca gets on my nerve sometimes and how much her uncle drives me nuts. But I didn't know what was really going on, I didn't know the pain she was suffering from nor the voices that she said spoke to her and directed her to do the unthinkable," explained Elaine.

"I really feel unprepared, and this isn't like me at all. But I have to know, what did she do? Why won't you just say it," said Morgan.

"Yes, I'm wondering myself... why don't you know any of this? Child, I understand this is fresh but you better get hip quick to some of these patients. Yes, some just need talking but some are way beyond that stage. Some are like Mariah. Hold on a second, is that the right time up there? Sheesh, I've been talking your ear off. How nice are you, you didn't even interrupt me not once? This is a really pretty facility. I'm in love with all the pretty colors. I bet it makes the patients feel happy inside. You guys have a lounge back there? Is that a pool table I see? I love the marble counter, and that fruit sure looks fresh. This tile floor is to die for. Your blue bobby pin is precious. Where'd you get that made, it looks like it's one of a kind," responded Elaine.

"Are you kidding me? I love that you're so observant but you're holding everything that happened right on the tip of your tongue. Why can't you just finish the story..." asked Morgan.

"I am, you are right. I was almost at the end. But isn't a part of your job knowing your subjects? Why don't you ask one of co-workers? Like I said the case made news everywhere. You should have a file handy somewhere. I think we've talked enough about it. I really just want to see my niece now if that's okay," urged Elaine.

"Yes of course, sorry I didn't mean to hound you. I know it's your actual life, the story was just getting really good that's all. I felt like we were reaching the climax and my interest spread like butter. Just plain old curiosity. I apologize for being inconsiderate. But as you've requested... *follow me please*," said Morgan.

"No need to be sorry honey it's fine. I'm used to it. I've been answering questions since the very beginning. I don't think there is a show or news outlet that hasn't asked me my take on things. It was a tragedy, that's how people react to tragedies," said Elaine.

"You mean like interviews?" asked Morgan.

"Well, what else would I mean you foolish woman. Yes interviews, and lots of them. I am the spokesperson for our family. When the lights came back on, I was the only one that didn't suffer from a shot. My sister was dead instantly and my brother in law died a few moments later. I was able to get the gun away from Mariah. She scratched me really good though. If you look close enough right here under my right eye, you can still see the mark. It's faint, but it's there. Luckily my husband and Rebecca ran outside to check for flashlights soon as the lights started to flicker. They didn't get shot at all. When they came back in Mariah was crying and she kept lying to them. She kept saying that I shot Evelyn and my brother in law and that I tried to shoot her too. She said that's why I had the gun. However, I tried to stop her but I was only able to save myself. When the police arrived, they searched her room and found her diary of notes and plans to kill us all. I was livid, but I couldn't show that. I knew then she needed serious help," said Elaine. "So, she killed them? That's why she's here? Well that don't make her crazy," said Morgan.

"But if you were listening at all child, I already told you what made her crazy," said Elaine.

"Yes, you did… so how did you all get away," asked Morgan. "Oh, my husband saved the day. He was the one that called the cops. Plus, we were okay once I managed to get the gun. We really just had to keep her there until they arrived. She didn't try to run," said Elaine.

"And what did you do Elaine? Not like that, I mean what did you do until help arrived?" asked Morgan. "I did what I've been doing her entire life, I helped. So… you do know more than I thought? Okay, we got into a scuffle. She didn't attempt to run but she did attack me. So I fought back. I wasn't going to end up like my sister. I knocked her in the head with the gun just enough so she'd fall asleep. When she woke up things were already taken care of. She was guilty before her case even happened. But I was able to get her a good lawyer that insisted it would be best to plead temporarily insanity. She was only going to stay in the first facility for five years but when I went for her checkup you know to see how she was progressing, I didn't see much of a difference. So, I asked for a stronger medicine and a little more time in the center. Pills can help, but the side effects sure don't. It's like every pill had a new effect. Some made her angry, some made her happy, and some made her violent. Fighting gives you more time. So that's how we get to where we are today. She can't stop fighting and writing these false stories about what happened. Seems like there isn't a strong enough drug to make her understand," said Elaine.

"Well what exactly is she understanding? It sounds like she was a sad kid that wanted her family together. Where does the murder scene come from? Why would she snap and leave you, your husband, and daughter all as witnesses?" asked Morgan.

"Kids are far better at communicating than we are Morgan. They're blunt! They will say things directly to us, and still we will decide to ignore them. Mariah was one of those kids, she said lots of things and no one wanted to listen. Like the weekend before Me, her, and her mom were hanging out at the grocery store you know the Piggly Wiggly just wasting time looking at things and spending money we really couldn't afford to spend. That's when shopping is fun you know rob Peter and pay Paul. That's what we did lots of times. Mariah was busy complaining as she always did – making her mama feel like a bad parent. So, to shut her up, she told her that it seems like her and her daddy can't do much right now but if something ever happened to them that Mariah would be set," said Elaine.

"Set? What's that mean!? How much was she talking!?" inquired Morgan.

"FIVE HUNDRED AND FIFTY-FIVE THOUSAND DOLLARS," replied Elaine.

"And she said this while you were there too?" asked Morgan. "That was my sister, we shared everything. There were no secrets. We looked up to each other. Of course, she said it while I was standing there. Why wouldn't she? Do you need help with what you're trying to say?" asked Elaine. "No ma'am again I'm only going based off of what you just said to me. That's a whole lot of money that's all. Since Mariah is here did it all go to her father's other children?" asked Morgan. "Money is nothing compared to family. Only a scum would be driven to harm their relative for a dollar," said Elaine.

"That's a lot more than a dollar but I totally agree. No amount of dollars is worth any life," Said Morgan. "And I tried to reach out to his other children but they never got back to me," said Elaine. "You were in charge of their legal affairs? How is that so? You're a lawyer?" asked Morgan. "I'm some of this and some of that. But to answer your question. Yes, I was in charge of the policies. I helped them pick everything in case of an emergency. I never thought it would come so soon. Mariah is still my family so I moved past her trying to kill me rather quickly. I worked with her lawyers in making decisions and I think we did a pretty good job," said Elaine.

"This is becoming one of my crime shows I used to watch with my mother. Okay so then ultimately what happened to the money? After all her fees and everything else where did the rest of their life insurance and other assets go?" asked Morgan.

"While setting the policies up my sister decided to be fairly generous. We *really* loved each other, but like all siblings we've had our brawls too. She told me that if anything should happen to her that I also wouldn't have to worry about anything. She said my only job would be to care for Mariah. But because of what Mariah did, the state took her and left me with the option of what to do," said Elaine. "The option of what to do with the money?" asked Morgan.

"Yes! Now I should go on in her room I can't stay long. I have tennis practice at 4," said Elaine.
"Yes ma'am…one more thing and I promise I'll let you go in and see her. Did you take Mariah's weakness and use it as your gain? Did you use the fact that she didn't feel loved and set her up? Did you kill her parents and frame her for it?" questioned Morgan.

"This isn't the first time Mariah has been relocated from one psychiatric center to the next. She does well for long periods, but every so often in between I guess because of the medicine, her mind really drifts off allowing her to write these creative and elaborate novellas. I think they start out as dreams, and she just runs with them. Like the one about her mother serving time in prison. Will you give me a break? That would never happen. She couldn't survive a cell if she tried. But that's Mariah, her mind takes her places. I love my niece but she doesn't have all of her marbles. If you actually talked to her you'd be able to tell," said Elaine.

"So, you're saying she is supposed to be here, and that she did commit a crime," asked Morgan. "Listen child if I go in this room right now and look at her notebook, I'm almost certain that I'll find wild fantasies about you, me, and whoever else she can pretend to be in order to carry out her script. These fictional stories allow her to escape reality. It's a coping mechanism. Just look up her file. I saw a session where she mentioned Mason Smith. Mason Smith is one of our neighbors. He went to school with Mariah and he never even looked her way. He liked the popular girls. He liked who Mariah wished she could be," said Elaine. "All of that could be absolutely true. She could struggle with identity issues. Maybe she really felt invisible. None of that means she had to hurt her parents. And I guess I told a little white lie. I did read one note. I read the note that said she knocked out and you were dead. The story that you both have told is closely related except you're still here. Why would she kill you? What did you do to her?" asked Morgan.

"I'm normally prepared for my speaking engagements. I feel like without being prepped I've done fairly well. Don't you think? You're still asking me about someone that has clinically been proven unfit to function properly in society on her own. I don't know what answer you want from me, but this is the only answer I have so, listen up. Mariah Shante Beauvoir has been in various facilities since the age of 16 after being proven guilty of murder. There were no twin sisters, boyfriends, fiancé, traveling to anywhere outside of her four walls. She's been a patient for more than half her life now. So, with that being said how can you have the audacity to question anything that I'm saying to you? I can prove everything. If you did your job I honestly wouldn't have to. What are you living in a bubble? How old are you again? This is the era of social media and technology; this story shouldn't be new to you. You shouldn't look so spaced out right now. At the end of the day all that matters is the verdict you know? An opinion never paid any of my bills, but that money sure helped. I can't tell you every piece of information that ran through her mind while firing that weapon. I didn't see her face or their reaction either for that matter. I just remember the cold, the quiet, the spookiness of the night. When the lights went out, the shots played hop scotch across their bodies. There weren't screams or aches of pleading and begging. Everything was still. The rain even paused. The window slowly slid back down and the damage that took place bled through the living room carpet. Scrabble spelled murder but didn't mention who. When the power came back on, I was able to get a grip again. I could see and although it seems that I could be just as likely, her lack of credibility was a sure clue. So, did I frame her for murder? No, I did not. Come on, I'm smarter than that. Why would I visit her? If I already have the money and she's stuck in here, what other reason would I need to keep in touch," said Elaine.

"Exactly, I think your story has a little imagination in it as well. See maybe you adored your sister. Maybe you admired her too. It's possible that you even looked up to her, but maybe the feeling wasn't so mutual. What if you did take their lives because you could never measure up to her standards? That would leave you with the one thing that did and a lump sum of money should anything HAPPEN to her. Except she's still here living and breathing and well that means you get nothing. And maybe that's why as crazy as it seems to portray you as such an envious backstabbing sister, it actually makes a little sense. Maybe she always knew you wanted what you couldn't have," said Morgan.

"Wow Morgan are you a writer too? I like that scenario. You could be right, but then again you could be wrong. Really can't be too sure huh? What if it's a mixture of both our ideas? Hmm anything is possible. Did I black out? Did she black out? Honestly who cares! But anyway, I'll let you go ahead and get back to work. You know what you're obligated to do, instead of harassing me. I think I can find my way from here. But I hope you enjoy the rest of your day Sugar…

Don't hurt yourself trying to solve an already solved mystery."

In Loving Memory of

my Auntie Barbara Harris.

I love you forever sugar...